The
Romance
Of
Winning
Children

The Romance Of Winning Children

BY
FRANK G. COLEMAN

UNION GOSPEL PRESS
CLEVELAND, OHIO

UNION GOSPEL PRESS, CLEVELAND, OHIO

The Romance Of Winning Children

This outstanding book is packed full of helpful, effective ideas to make winning children to the Lord a successful and rewarding experience.

The author begins with a discussion of the importance of winning children while they are young. He explains the process of leading a child to Christ.

He then offers helpful suggestions on telling stories, leading songs, using visual aids, teaching memory work, and handling discipline problems.

This is a book that every teacher will want to read. Anyone who works with children will find it profitable and inspiring.

Hundreds of workable ideas for winning children to Christ . . .

effective methods offered by a veteran in child evangelism, Frank G. Coleman.

PREFACE

"The Romance of Winning Children" is presented in a most effective and practical manner in this volume. The author has given careful consideration to the many aspects of the child, his need, and God's provision for that need. The methods which the author proposes have proved very successful.

This book is worthy of careful study. It commands our every talent and close attention. By means of the assistance offered, let us seek to become proficient and efficient in leading boys and girls to the Saviour and in teaching them to live for God.

The child presents great potentialities and in these pages effective ways of developing them are given. The consideration of the message of this book will stir the heart and mind to see and grasp the wonderful opportunities offered in winning children for our Lord Jesus Christ.

Walter L. Wilson, M.D., L.H.D.

CONTENTS

Chapter I.

THE CHILD AND THE WORD

"Even so it is not the will of your Father which is in heaven, that one of these little ones should perish" (Matt. 18:14). The Lord is interested in the winning of children, while they are children.

There are many who do not believe that children can be genuinely converted and born again. Almost invariably, when children respond to an invitation in evangelistic meetings, there are those who discount their action by saying that they do not know what they are doing. In some instances, it is doubtless true that they do not comprehend; but in far more cases than most of us believe, or care to admit, they do grasp very clearly their need, God's answer to that need in Christ, and the reality of their own appropriation of Him as their personal Saviour. Were we to see removed from the active membership of the Christian church those who so received Christ in childhood, we should soon see the closing of many a church door.

Some say that a child should be left to decide in his more mature years whether or not he will accept the Lord as his Saviour. Let him grow up unbiased and when he is in his late teens or early twenties he can decide. This sounds plausible, but it is utter folly. No child can grow up unbiased in our day. If the children are not biased strongly for Christ, they will be biased as strongly against Him. They breathe the very atmosphere of godless unbelief even in the most ordinary of their childhood pursuits. No child should be left to grow up in our world of unbelief and flagrant sin without having heard the gospel with a persuasive invitation to believe it and accept its salvation.

"But," you may say, "can a child grasp the meaning and intent of the gospel?" Why not? Is not a child that is old enough knowingly to sin also old enough savingly to believe? At what age can a child experience the conscious guilt of sin? At what age can a child hear that God is, and having heard, believe it? At what age can a child hear that a person lived and died in time past and accept it as a fact? At that same age, he can hear and believe that God came down in the Person of His Son to die and rise again, that that child's own sin might be removed if he will believe. Spurgeon once said, "A child of five, if properly instructed, can as truly believe and be regenerated as any adult."

The truth of the matter is that countless thousands of children have heard the gospel, have savingly believed in Christ, and have gone on to give ample evidence of regeneration in useful Christian lives of service. Call the roll of the saints of God who have led the forces of the church, who have pioneered in world missions, who have taught the people about God. The vast majority of them were saved in childhood.

Matthew Henry was saved at eleven, Dr. Watts at nine, Jonathan Edwards at eight, Richard Baxter at six. Polycarp was no more than nine years old when he received Christ, and for eighty-six years served Him faithfully. Spurgeon, soon after he was twelve years old, asked permission of his family to visit different churches. Though his father and grandfather were ministers of the gospel, he was seeking someone who could tell him how to be freed from the burden of sin he was then feeling so acutely. Perhaps that is why he became a prophet of child evangelism in his day. Count Zinzendorf, leade. of the Moravians, at the age of four, signed his name to this covenant of his own composition: "Dear Saviour, do Thou be mine and I will be Thine." Lord Shaftesbury attributed his decision for Christ to a Christian nurse who told him of the Saviour when he was scarcely past infancy. C. A. Benson, in his *Introduction to Child Study* said, "Out of 71 corporate members of the American Board of Missions, 19 stated they were converted at so early an age that they were unable to remember." Lady Dobby, wife of the famed

Defender of Malta, once said that as far back as she could remember she knew of no time when she did not believe in Christ as her Saviour, and that she must have been evangelized and led to accept Christ by her mother, perhaps through a picture, near the tender age of three!

We older ones have a gospel which is the power of God unto salvation to those who believe it. We have believed it for ourselves and so have experienced its power. But our own faith in the gospel does not end the matter. As we receive it for ourselves, we also receive it as a trust for others who shall believe through our word, both young and old. The Word of God sets no age limit on faith. Christ in His finished work is for the boys and girls as well as for the graybeards. Why, then, should Christian people, while believing that the gospel is God's power when given to the old, refuse to believe that it is equally His power when given to the young?

Why, of course! Did not our Lord say, "I thank thee, O Father, Lord of heaven and earth, because thou hast hid these things from the wise and the prudent, and hast revealed them unto babes" (Matt. 11:25)? Did He not say, "Out of the mouth of babes and sucklings thou hast perfected praise" (Matt. 21:16)? Was He not holding a little child in His arms when He said, "These little ones which believe in me" (Matt. 18:6)?

Consider the discourse on the little child from which the last quoted words are taken.

MATTHEW 18:1-14

The subject of our Lord's discourse is the little child. How little? Mark gives us a clue when he tells us that he was nestled in the arms of the Lord. He could hardly have been much more than a toddler. One does not hold any but a small child during such a discourse.

The occasion grew out of the selfish and prideful question of personal pre-eminence among the disciples, but apart from a very brief answer to the question about which they were squabbling, all that He says in the passage is about the child in His arms. Far more than they needed to understand their individual place and prominence in the kingdom, did they need to know the place and the value of the child in the gracious plans and purposes of God.

There are no less than eight important statements about the child made in the Lord's sermon which every Christian should ponder well.

Conversion occurs on the child's level (18:3). To all intents and purposes it would appear that most Christians regard conversion as something of an adult experience to which spiritually precocious children may rise on rare occasions. But it is not so in this word of the Lord. Conversion is not only possible for the child, but any adult who would enter the kingdom of heaven must become as a little child! Children are not saved in an adult fashion, but rather it is the other way around! The child, because he is a child, is already on the level where conversion is an ever-present possibility, needing only the presentation and the acceptance of the facts. All others must stoop to enter. No adult is ever saved who does not come in childlike simplicity and trust, re-entering the state out of which he has grown and which he tends to discount.

Humbleness, the essential quality of kingdom greatness, is already the child's portion (18:4). It is not so much humility of spirit that is in view here. It is rather a humble state of weakness and dependence which determines greatness. Even a child can be proud; and the older we grow the more proud we become. What humility of spirit it takes to admit our childish weakness and utter dependence upon the Lord when we come to Him in adult years! The child who is brought into a saving relationship with Him, who is led along the way of growth in grace in his early years, seldom abandons his humble dependence.

To receive a child in the Name of the Lord Jesus is to receive the Lord Himself (18:5). No blessing is more quickly realized than this in the experience of the soul-winner working among children. The gracious presence of the Lord is never more keenly realized than in the hallowed moments when He is entering the heart of a child to take up His abode. In a sacred and uniquely blessed way He manifests Himself to the children's evangelist. This is the almost universal testimony of those who are at work winning the children to Him.

The little child can believe in Christ (18:6). "These little ones which believe in me," the Master said. That should settle the question as to whether a child can be saved. Remember that it was a little child, small enough to be held in the Speaker's arms. "Whom shall he teach knowledge?" asks Isaiah (Isa. 28:9), "and whom shall he make to understand doctrine?" The answer is immediately given, "Them that are weaned from the milk, and drawn from the breasts." A child old enough to hear a bedtime story is old enough to hear of the Saviour and His finished work, and in hearing, can believe in Him. There is no other construction to be placed on the Master's words than this, that a child can believe in Christ. Let us not evade it; His words are clear and plain.

To cause a child to stumble is to deserve death and hell (18:6, 8). He that offends or causes a little child to stumble ought to be drowned. He ought to be cast into hell fire. This is the Lord's statement of the seriousness of sinning against the child. Fortunately for us older ones, He is a God of grace and deals with us not on the basis of our just deserts, but on the basis of Calvary. How many there are who have put off the inquiring little one whose concern about his soul was veiled by his childish ways! How many children have been denied the word of the gospel by some parent or teacher, only to grow up without Christ, finally to die without Him. Is it not a serious matter? Are not the issues heaven and hell?

To undervalue the child is to miss God's evaluation, for children are the objects of heavenly concern (18:10). God places a premium upon the souls of boys and girls. Someone has said that "they have front seats in heaven." Whatever may be the full meaning of this passage, it at least gives us the mind of the Lord in the matter. So precious are they that "their angels do always behold the face of my Father which is in heaven." And we tend to undervalue them, even to the point of counting their conversion a thing of little present importance. Great emphasis is laid upon the conversion of the seventy-year-old sinner, while youngsters are passed by with the expression, "They are only children." But the youngster has a life of service before him, while the older convert has only a wasted life behind him. When an evangelist was asked about the numerical results of a certain service he replied, "Three and a half were saved." "Oh," his interested friend said, "three adults and a child." "No," the answer was, "three children and an adult." Do not undervalue the little ones who come to Christ.

The child should be sought as the shepherd seeks the stray sheep (18:12-13). Commonly, these verses are interpreted as meaning adult sinners; however, the preceding verses all refer to the child, and likewise, the verse that follows speaks of "one of these little ones" which he was holding. By every law of interpretation, the child is also meant in the parable of the lost sheep. That children should be sought and found as straying sheep may not be the entire meaning, but it is certainly the first application that should be made in light of the context in which the parable appears.

It is not the Father's will that a single child should perish (18:14). Here is a promise that is clear and plain, a plain statement that makes possible prevailing prayer, for we know that He hears and that we will so have the petition granted (I John 5:14-15). True, the expression is a negative one. Is it not so placed that we should not presume? How many would prevail in prayer for the soul of a child were it stated in the positive? As it is, we are all too prone to take refuge from our own responsibility by hiding behind the will of God. Let us take this expression of the Father's will at its face value and claim it in complete readiness to do what He may direct so that boys and girls may be brought to a saving knowledge of His Son.

CHILDHOOD—THE BELIEVING AGE

Evangelism among children is a more fruitful ministry than evangelism among those of any other age. Reuben Archer Torrey said, "It is almost the easiest thing in the world to lead a child from five to ten years of age to a definite acceptance of Christ. It is much harder to lead a child between ten and fifteen years to Christ; but it is easier to lead a child between ten and fifteen years to Christ than a young person between the ages of twenty and twenty-five. The younger you can begin with the children to lead them to make an actual acceptance of Christ, the easier the work will be, and the more satisfactory."

Childhood is the age of dependence and trust. These are the years when children are utterly dependent upon their elders for the supply of their needs. The child looks in faith to human parents for food, shelter, clothing, and for those little delights that brighten early years. These are the days when even knowledge comes because the child believes his elders. Hardly a waking hour passes in which faith is not exercised. True, it is faith placed in human friends, in human counselors, but it is faith. There is but one kind of faith; the distinction is in faith's objects.

What an opportune time to fasten the child's native faith eternally upon a Saviour who can supremely answer to his simple trust. Skepticism has not yet dominated the scene and does not stand in the way of his believing in Christ. It is as natural for a child to trust in his Saviour when told of His work as it is for him to believe in the goodness of a relative of whom he has been told, but whom he has never seen. In the days of the Lord Jesus Christ it was true that the children believed on Him (Matt. 18:6). It can still be true today.

CHILDHOOD—THE SENSITIVE AGE

The heart of a child is exceedingly tender. Conscience is never keener than in childhood. Indeed, it would seem that the history of growth and development is one of a gradual hardening of heart. The conscience, unless quickened by Christ, becomes calloused by degrees until, in unbelieving old age, there is seldom any distress of heart and mind in the normal end of a sinful life. As the years come and go, people become more and more insensitive to sin. This is a fact of life that can be seen on every hand. But in childhood it is not so.

Sin is real to boys and girls of tender years. It is distressing to them. They lie awake many times with troublesome questionings seething within them. They know by their very moral make-up when sin makes an entrance into their lives, and they sense their guilt. Perhaps they cannot put it into words, but the sense of guilt is there just the same.

A sense of guilt can overwhelm a young child. So true is this fact, that modern psychiatry in treating many cases brought to its attention will search for the cause of guilt in order to effect a cure. We are told that some of the nervous and mental disorders that call for the work of the psychiatrist are due to a sense of guilt incurred in childhood. This feeling of guilt remains long after the incident that aroused it has been forgotten. It colors the whole life by manifesting itself later in many and devious ways, not as guilt, but as fear, worry, depression and despondency, or any of a whole host of mental and emotional derangements, all of which disappear with the uncovering of the long-forgotten feeling of guilt.

One of many such cases handled by a present-day specialist was that of an attorney who had been beset by worries for years. He realized that they were groundless and tried to stop his worrying; but worries are not cast out by self-determination alone. He finally worried about his worrying and practically had to give up his work. His worry proved to be caused by a boyish escapade that had given him a lasting, though not consciously realized, feeling of guilt. The feeling remained, even though the escapade apparently was soon forgotten. It cropped out in strange and unwarranted worries for many years afterwards. The worries remained, despite sincere efforts to stop them, until the specialist ferreted out the feeling of guilt where the attorney could face it intelligently. Any psychiatrist could cite similar instances almost without number.

Christian workers may not appreciate the reality of sin in a child's life, but the psychiatrist does. He knows that childhood sin and guilt are stern realities. What a service the children's evangelist can perform in the light of this fact!

We have a gospel that deals with sin, attacking both its root and its fruit. If a child can feel guilt, can he not likewise know forgiveness? It is unthinkable that God should so constitute a child in his spiritual being that he may suffer under the burden of his sin, without also including him in the company of those who may benefit from the sacrifice of Christ. If the child has the capacity to sin and realize in himself sin's fruitage of guilt and shame, surely a God of love would not deny him the capacity for receiving the gospel and its eternal blessings.

The tender heart of a child responds to the poignant story of the sufferings of Christ for sin. The cruelty of the cross is meaningful to the little one and he sees Calvary in all its hideousness as caused by human sin when the gospel is faithfully presented to him. He also comprehends the love of God in taking sin upon Himself in the Person of His Son. Sensitive to sin, the child is equally sensitive to love. The child can understand the meaning of Calvary.

CHILDHOOD—THE AFFECTIONATE AGE

Children are creatures of love. They respond to it wholeheartedly. They are ready to fasten their affections upon any person who gives the least indication of interest in them. And this is a day so busy and so full of hustle and bustle that many are growing up starved for the affection that is their due. Especially is this true in recent years when the changing scene has brought such a change in the home life of the family. Many children are often made to feel that they are in the way.

Today's child will respond to the love of Christ, if he but knows of it. For years the Wordless Book, perhaps the most blessed gospel object lesson of modern times, was used without any unusual success. The early use of the object was to begin with the black page and present the facts concerning sin and guilt and punishment, then to proceed to the red page and the finished work of Christ, then on to the white page which stands for the cleansing that comes through receiving Him, finishing with the gold page and its accompanying message about heaven. Then the approach was changed. Instead of beginning with the fact of sin, workers began to present heaven and the love of God first of all. The results were immediately overwhelming. Little hungry hearts answered at once to the love of God. The fact of sin became highlighted by that love. The blood of Christ became all the more precious and understandable as a revelation of love. Children are hungry for love. They respond to the love of God if they are told that He loves them and are shown what He has done for them.

Be sure of this, that whatever the unreached child knows about God, he little suspects that He is Love. Others have told him of God's readiness to punish, perhaps. He may have been presented as a force or power. You alone, a child of God, can tell the child that God loves him, and that for love of him, He sent His only-begotten Son into the world to take the punishment for his sin that he might be freely forgiven. That children will respond to this love has been demonstrated again and again and again. Glory in the fact and use it to the winning of young hearts.

CHILDHOOD—THE TEACHABLE AGE

Children are teachable. Childhood is the age of learning things. It is the inquisitive age. His trust in human teachers makes possible the child's acquiring a body of formal knowledge, most of which he receives by faith rather than by experimentation. Minds are never so alert, memories never so retentive, as at this time. How much we learn in the first few years of life! This is the time to teach eternal things—to bring that young life to the eternal Teacher of eternal things, who alone can instruct in the things of God.

It is asked, "Can the child understand the plan of redemption and related spiritual truth?" It isn't a matter of understanding but of faith. No one can understand these things in any great measure, but he can believe them. "O the depth of the riches both of the wisdom and knowledge of God! how unsearchable are His judgments, and His ways past finding out!" The child, in his secular education, is given an increasing body of facts to be believed. Understanding, that is, the seeing of the facts in their inter-relationships, comes later. Facts of any kind can be received by anyone, young or old, if his vocabulary contains words that will set them forth to him. Salvation comes by believing historical facts, and by receiving a historical Person, the Lord Jesus Christ. The facts and the Person can be set forth in words that even the very young know. Salvation is by faith, understanding may come later.

Let there be no mistake here. We are discussing the entrance into the Christian life, not development in the Christian life. The teaching under discussion is that of the initial things. Do not make the mistake of subjecting the child to an indeterminate course of Christian education in the mistaken hope that at some future time he will know enough and understand enough to become a Christian. Growth in knowledge follows acceptance of Christ; it can never precede. "The natural man receiveth not the things of the Spirit of God: for they are foolishness unto him: neither can he know them, because they are spiritually discerned" (I Cor. 2:14). But once the Spirit of God enters, then there can be true reception of divine truth and an accompanying growth and development. Lead the child to the Lord at the beginning, and his teachable years become spiritually profitable.

In the plastic, receptive years is the time of opportunity for the pastor, for the teacher of a Sunday School class, for the Bible Club leader, for the parent. Let the opportunity pass, for it will pass all too soon, and other influences will sway the hearts and minds of the youngsters. It will become more and more difficult to get them to attend to the Word of God. We lose contact with many of the boys and girls of our Sunday Schools during their teens. We have failed to establish them in Christ in the opportune season of childhood, and youth finds them away from our influence. They may be lost forever. It is a solemn and heart-searching thought that should move us to grasp every opportunity to win the children for the Saviour.

WHAT HAPPENS WHEN A THOROUGHLY EVANGELIZED CHILD BELIEVES?

First, a yellow caution light or two.

The child who is thoroughly evangelized and believes in Christ is regenerated. He is born again. All that occurs at regeneration occurs in his case. However, the outward manifestations and the inward feelings are not the same in all cases of conversion. It is foolish to insist that the child shall react in the way that the adult does. The things attendant upon the regeneration of a child of seven are quite different from the sinner who, after seventy years of sin, gives up to the claims of Christ. One of a board of deacons, examining a child candidate for baptism, was alarmed that the eight-year-old lass was shedding no tears of repentance. "She doesn't seem to know anything about the 'slough of despond,'" he said in her hearing. "Oh, I didn't come that way," was her answer. Let us not demand of the child the same feelings that an older person may have in such an experience.

Of the many mistakes that have been made in the matter of bringing children to a saving knowledge of Christ, none is more disastrous in its end results than that of expecting too much of the young Christian child. It is often fatal to the natural spiritual development of such a two-fold babe in Christ. Saved children are still children in their outlook and behavior. We should expect fruitage and should look for development in grace, but let us not lose sight of the fact that children may be truly born-again Christians without having reached a very high level of practical sanctification. It will come, but in its due season.

What, then, does happen when a child fully believes in Christ after he has been faithfully and thoroughly evangelized? We say "thoroughly evangelized" because so much emphasis is placed on bringing the child to Calvary that it is sometimes thought that child evangelism enthusiasts end the matter with the single result of bringing the child to accept Christ as his Saviour. Nothing could be further from the truth. Thorough evangelization, as we shall see, goes deeper than that.

First of all, he turns to Christ as Saviour and Friend. Secondly, and here is where thorough evangelization comes in, he turns to Christ as Lord and Helper. Thorough evangelization does not end with Calvary and forgiveness of sin, but goes on to the empty tomb and the life of obedience and power.

When the time comes that the child is conscious of the fact that he is a sinner before God, having sensed his own guilt and having been brought under conviction of sin through the Word, the picture of Christ on the cross bearing our sins should be presented to him. The love of Christ in dying for sinners and the love of God in sending His Son to die for us should be emphasized. Three texts— John 3:16, I Peter 2:24, and I John 1:9—should be given to him so that he may memorize them and repeat them every time he does wrong after his conversion. When Christ is presented so as Saviour, the child, in his voluntary act of turning to Him, turns to Him as Saviour. But there is the further fact that his Saviour is also his Friend. The child can grasp this. He has troubles. His troubles are as real to him as ours are to us. He needs the Friend of children. As the Lord Jesus is presented to children as Saviour and Friend, they are able to come to Him in an intensely practical way.

If evangelization is thorough, it will include the presentation of Christ as Lord and Helper of the saved boy and girl. No child should be permitted to leave the presence of the Christian worker until he is pointed along the way of obedience to the Master. There is no true love for Christ without the willingness to obey Him. The child must be led to see this, that his start in the Christian life may be in the right direction. He needs help from above from the time that he becomes a Christian. How much help he gets from Christ in the future may be determined by our faithfulness in this point. In the conversion of the child there is a wholehearted willingness to do all that is needful. The thoroughly evangelized child turns to Christ as Saviour and Friend and yields to Him as Lord and Helper. There need be no very remarkable experience in all this. Often in waiting for what they call "the change," parents and teachers neglect to lead the child to Christ after this full manner so that the change may be possible.

What are the results of such a reception of Christ? The child loves Christ with a love that can only increase with the years. Love is natural to childhood. A child can love Christ with all the intensity of his heart. The child will know Christ with an ever increasing knowledge. Adults often have difficulty in knowing Christ intimately, but it is not difficult for the child. He becomes very, very real and very, very personal, and ever present to the child. The child will begin to trust Christ with an unfaltering trust. The child knows what it is to trust father and mother. He lives on the level of trust every day. Jesus has paid the penalty for sin. There is no more work to be done in giving him a right to come to God. The child who is taught to take Jesus absolutely at His Word and trust Him for salvation and for those things which accompany salvation will do so without hesitation. Then there is obedience. Trust cannot be seen, but obedience is evident, and it is the effect of trust. The child must be taught this at the outset that his beginning may be complete. It must be repeated again and again until his obedience proves his faith.

All that we have said thus far is said as we look at the human side. Let us look at the divine side briefly. When a child believes in Christ with saving faith, everything occurs that occurs in the case of any other person who believes. He becomes the subject of grace. He is numbered among the elect. He has experienced repentance and faith. He is converted. He is joined with Christ in an indissoluble union. He is justified. He is born again. He is adopted into the family of God. God begins a work in him that He has pledged Himself to complete. The Holy Spirit takes up His abode in the child to become his Comforter, his Teacher, his Enabler.

The sum of a child's believing in Christ, upon his having been thoroughly evangelized, is that he turns to Christ as Saviour and Friend, as Lord and Helper; that he may love Him, know Him, trust Him, obey Him; and that God in turn fulfills His covenant with the believing child.

Children can be saved. The gospel message should not be denied to them. We have a message which they can receive. The operations of God are the same for them as for others. It is not His will that one of them should perish. Shall we not, then, put ourselves to the work of evangelizing the world of children for whom also Christ died?

Chapter II.

THE CHILD AND YOU

It is impossible for any child of God to say truthfully, "I cannot be used to win a child to Christ." Children can be evangelized. You can be an evangelist to them, provided of course that you know the Lord Jesus Christ as your Saviour. The things that are needful are all within your grasp. God has placed no requirements before you that you are unable to fulfill. A great many Christians regard the winning of children as a highly specialized ministry, demanding the services of a "children's expert." The simple truth is that any yielded saint can be an effective soul-winner among the boys and girls if he will take God's way. God, in His infinite wisdom in providing for mankind's redemption, has also provided that men shall make known His salvation to men, and has equipped them with natural endowments and stands ready to supply their spiritual need so that they may be fitted to make Christ known to others. The means are available to all and the conditions may be met by all.

Naturally, there are requirements. God would use clean vessels; He would use prepared instruments. No soul-winning ministry should be entered thoughtlessly and blindly. Particularly is this true in child evangelism. There are certain prerequisites. This does not mean, however, that a long course of study and intensive preparation are demanded before this fruitful ministry may be undertaken. Study and preparation, of course, are called for if one is to be increasingly used; but do not go astray at this point. To do the work of child evangelism requires no elaborate training or equipment at the outset beyond a real born-again experience in the life, a vision of the need, a surrendered life, prayer, and a Bible used under the direction of the Holy Spirit. However, there are helps and training available for all who feel the need and the desire—for assistance grows with the experience of the child evangelist. More and more, volunteer workers are realizing that evangelism of children, particularly of those whose home life gives them no Christian background, calls for methods suited exactly to these boys and girls. But the basic prerequisites are not beyond your power to fulfill immediately.

Willingness.

First there must be willingness. The first question is not "Can I do it?" nor even "How shall I go about it?" but "Am I willing to lead a child to Christ?" A willing mind is what God desires, and it is that which He blesses before all else. "If any man will do his will, he shall know" (John 7:17), is the foundation for training in all Christian work. If you are not willing to lead a child to Christ in God's way, it is useless to attempt it. Your will must be wholly resigned in this matter.

Knowledge.

Knowledge comes next. Willingness must be followed by a certain knowledge. "Study to shew thyself approved unto God, a workman that needeth not to be ashamed" (II Tim. 2:15). You must know Christ. You must know your Bible. You must know yourself. You must know the child.

Without a personal knowledge of Christ in salvation, nothing can be accomplished no matter how much effort you put forth. Ye must be born again. All knowledge in spiritual things begins with a new birth through a personal appropriation of the sacrifice of Christ. Little can be the result if, beyond a knowledge of Him in salvation, there is not also an intimate, day-by-day fellowship with Him. The more you know Him, the better you will be able to present Him to the child, and the more you will have the desire to do it. You must know Christ.

You must know your Bible. It is not enough to know that a certain thought is expressed somewhere and somehow in the Scriptures. You must know the passage. You should be able to repeat the verse, or at the very least, be able to turn to it that it might be identified in the mind of the child as being the very Word of God. It is not necessary to know the entire Bible by chapter and verse, but however limited your education in the Scriptures may be, there are some passages which you must know. And you must know them for yourself, having experienced their truth in your own actual appropriation of them, before you can hope to teach them to others. A working knowledge of the Sword of the Spirit is not to be dispensed with. You must know the Word of God.

You must know yourself. How few of us see ourselves as others see us! Some cannot lead a soul to Christ because they repel others. Curtness, abruptness, an unloving attitude will not win souls. Vinegar doesn't draw butterflies. Study yourself that you may mend the ways which are unattractive and that stand in the way of greater usefulness. "Know thyself."

You must know the child. Children are not led to Christ en masse, but individually. However much you may be able to learn of child psychology, crowd psychology, and platform methods, so that you may move an entire audience of children to action, it is still true that salvation is an individual matter with each one. You cannot win a group of children unless you win each child individually. You must think in terms of the individual child. You should study each child as fully as circumstances permit. Do that and you will know "children." Especially is this demanded if your contact with the child is more or less a continuing one. You should try to find the particular viewpoint of each one. You should know what it is that he knows, what he dislikes, what he likes. You must get acquainted with the individual child as intimately as you can. Study him closely.

Dedication.

To willingness and a measure of knowledge must be added complete dedication. It is your body with all its faculties that God would have you present to Him (Rom. 12:1). Only that which you yield to Him can be fully used by Him in this great work. Let Him have yourself completely, that He may fill you with His Spirit and use you to the fullest extent.

Power.

There must be power in addition to all this, and in all this. The power is spiritual. This work is not to be done in your power, but in His. Let the Holy Spirit do His work through you. You can have as much power as you are willing to use for the glory of God. Without it you are helpless. With it you can do "all things." The three things that release the power of the Spirit are within your possibilities. They are prayer, connection with the Source—God, and use of the power given.

These are the prerequisites to soul-winning among the children. None of them is denied to you. You may have them all if you will, and you may have them without delay.

GOD'S PROVISIONS FOR YOUR SUCCESS

Have you ever thought how full indeed is the marvelous provision God has made for your success in winning the boys and girls? Consider all the things that stand in your favor as you undertake the evangelization of the young.

The Gospel.

The gospel itself stands in your favor as a winner of children. We need to keep in mind some essential facts about the gospel by which we are saved. We little realize sometimes just how much is comprehended in it. Ask God to give you a new appreciation of the gospel, its facts and its power.

The gospel is good news (Luke 2:10-11, 31-32). It is light in a dark place. It brings a message of glad tidings to the heart that is downcast with the weight of sin. The gospel is the power of God (Rom. 1:16; I Cor. 1:18; I Thess. 1:5). Nothing is more powerful. You have at your disposal that which casts down strongholds, works miracles, changes hearts and minds. The message that you are called upon to give to boys and girls is its own power. We who give it out are only channels. The gospel is to be preached to every creature (Mark 16:15). The gospel brings peace (Luke 2:10, 14; Eph. 6:15). The gospel brings hope (Col. 1:23). We should not be ashamed of it (Rom. 1:16; II Tim. 1:8). All these facts are true of the message we bear.

The gospel is utter simplicity. It is not only ideally suited to the needs of every child, but there is no idea contained in it that is beyond a child's comprehension. It is so simple that it can be summarized in a single sentence. Indeed, it has been done by one who appreciated its power: "How that Christ died for our sins according to the scriptures; and that he was buried, and that he rose again the third day according to the scriptures" (I Cor. 15:3-4). When any person, however young, lays hold on this simple threefold fact, in that instant he is saved. For this gospel, so simply stated that a child can receive it, is "the power of God unto salvation to every one that believeth" (Rom. 1:16).

Put these two verses together, this one sentence statement of the gospel, and the statement in Romans. There are but four very simple ideas to be received:

1. Christ died for our sins. He took our punishment. Before God, He received the wages of sin in our place.

2. He was buried. His death was an actual death. He did not simulate death, nor faint away. He really died.

3. He rose again. He lives! He has the power to save us from sin. He is a living personal Saviour whom God has approved by raising Him from the dead.

4. Receiving Him in these regards, through simple faith, brings the miracle of salvation, with all that is involved in it, into our lives.

None of these ideas is too much for a child of grade-school age to grasp. Children as young as three have grasped them, and they were not unusually precocious. Boys and girls are saved when, seeing their need of a Saviour from sin, they believe this gospel and receive the Lord Jesus Christ as their own personal Saviour. The gospel is in your favor! Give it to the child of your home, of your neighborhood, of your church and Sunday School. It is not above them; it is for them.

Warning!

Once and again we would issue a warning lest we go astray in the spiritual education of the young—that even in the child's acquisitive period of learning things, there can be no growth in grace and in the knowledge of the Lord and Saviour Jesus Christ until the child has been brought into an experience of that grace through the knowledge of the Christ of Calvary and the empty tomb. Here is where we have erred in time past. Our procedure has been to impose upon the child a sustained diet of Bible history and morality, under the assumption that at some indeterminate future time he may acquire enough Bible knowledge to go through the process of getting saved, automatically or otherwise!

It is little wonder that many of our Sunday School boys and girls, to look at a typical result of our historical approach, never take a stand for Christ and never come into the membership of the church. The natural man, even though a child, rebels against the things of God; and the mind of the flesh is enmity with Him even when that natural mind belongs to a pink-cheeked child. We must evangelize in order to teach in any true, Scriptural sense, even in the acquisitive age of learning things.

Let us remind ourselves that it is the Holy Spirit who teaches and not we ourselves. He does it through us, of course; but it is His work and it is our responsibility to permit Him to do it through the Word as we give it out. He reveals the things of God (I Cor. 2:10, 13). He brings

the words of Christ to remembrance (John 14:26). He
directs in the way of Godliness (Isa. 30:21; Ezek. 36:27).
He enables His witnesses to teach (I Cor. 12:8). He guides
into all truth (John 14:26; John 16:13). Let Him do His
work through you. Depend upon Him. Make certain that
the child has become the residence of the Holy Spirit
through personal faith in Christ.

If the people of God were to place the proper emphasis
upon the evangelizing of the boys and girls, if every boy
and girl in every Christian home, in every Sunday School
class, in every week-day Bible class were to be faced continually with the necessity of personally receiving Christ
as Saviour, we should soon see our Sunday Schools crowding out their quarters. Many of our Sunday Schools could
be doubled in a few months if the normal Sunday-to-Sun-
day gains would be conserved. The evangelizing of the
children is the way of conservation.

The Holy Spirit Works Through You.

The work of the Holy Spirit is through the yielded
people of God. He has no hands but your hands, no lips
but yours, no voice but yours. The work of child evangelism is God's work through you by the working of His
Spirit. All evangelism is the work of God by His Holy
Spirit. As you permit Him to minister Christ to the unsaved, He does so. But your yieldedness is essential to His
working. It is comforting to know that we have not been
left alone to work conviction of sin and faith in Christ by
our own power and wisdom. The promise is, "Ye shall receive power, after that the Holy Ghost is come upon you:
and ye shall be witnesses unto me" (Acts 1:8).

All too many of the Lord's people have the mistaken
idea that it is one's schooling, debating ability, public
speaking aptitude, persuasiveness of speech, or any of the
many qualities we see and admire in the more gifted that
is needful to win a soul to Christ. The exact opposite is
true. These things are good. They are desirable. We ought
to cultivate them. But they are not the vital things. Would

that we were all gifted with them, but God designs to use the baser things first of all.

Every children's worker should examine the ministry of the Apostle Paul as described in I Corinthians 2:1-5: "And I, brethren, when I came to you, came not with excellency of speech or of wisdom, declaring unto you the testimony of God. For I determined not to know any thing among you, save Jesus Christ, and him crucified. And I was with you in weakness, and in fear, and in much trembling. And my speech and my preaching was not with enticing words of man's wisdom, but in demonstration of the Spirit and of power: that your faith should not stand in the wisdom of men, but in the power of God."

This is the kind of witnessing that God honors. To depend on anything but His power is to fail. God can use the humblest saint to win a child if he will but open wide his whole being and become a channel for the power of God. It is every Christian's privilege to witness to children in the power of the Holy Spirit. That we may fully appreciate the work of the Holy Spirit, let us look at some things that are His to do, remembering that these are His tasks and not our own, and that He does them as we permit Him to use and control us in whom He dwells.

He strives with sinners (Gen. 6:3). He reproves (John 16:8). He helps our infirmities (Rom. 8:26). He teaches (John 14:26; I Cor. 12:3). He guides (John 16:13). He testifies of Christ (John 15:26). He glorifies Christ (John 16:14). He has a power of His own (Rom. 15:13). He searches all things (Rom. 11:33-34; I Cor. 2:10-11). These are His to do.

Our great failure in all soul-winning has often had this at its roots, that we failed to realize that the winning of souls, whether old or young, is the work of God. It depends entirely upon the working of God by His Spirit through His Word given through us. Once we see this simple truth and, recognizing it as applicable to our ministry to childhood, go forth as His witnesses to them, we shall soon have the knowledge born of experience that children can receive the gospel and be born again.

The Word of God.

In your favor also is the Word of God, the Spirit's Sword. It "is quick, and powerful, and sharper than any twoedged sword, piercing even to the dividing asunder of soul and spirit, and of the joints and marrow, and is a discerner of the thoughts and intents of the heart" (Heb. 4:12). The Word is able to make wise unto salvation (II Tim. 3:15). It regenerates (I Pet. 1:23). It makes alive (Ps. 119:50, 93). It illuminates (Ps. 119:130). It converts (Ps. 19:7). It produces faith (John 20:31). It cleanses the heart (John 15:3; Eph. 5:26). It cleanses the ways (Ps. 119:9). The Word works effectually in them that believe (I Thess. 2:13).

The Promises of God.

It is to the promises of God that the child evangelist must turn at all times. On them he must rest, or he will fail. The promises concerning the Holy Spirit, the promises concerning child evangelism, those concerning the Word, these are the realities that our faith must grasp and hold with unshakeable confidence.

Have you thought of God's promises—what is involved in the making of them, your receiving and resting upon them, and God's fulfillment of them? They are made in Christ (Eph. 3:6; II Tim. 1:1). God is faithful to fulfill them (Titus 1:2; Heb. 10:23). God remembers them (Ps. 105:42; Luke 1:54-55). They are good (I Kings 8:56). They are holy (Ps. 105:42). They are exceeding great and precious (II Pet. 1:4). They are confirmed in Christ (Rom. 15:8). In Him they are yea and amen (II Cor. 1:20). They come to us through the righteousness of faith (Rom. 4:13, 16). They are obtained through faith (Heb. 11:33). They are given to those who believe (Gal. 3:22). They are inherited through faith and patience (Heb. 6:12, 15; 10:36). They will be performed in due season (Jer. 33:14;

Acts 7:17; Gal. 4:4). Not one shall fail (Josh. 23:14; I Kings 8:56). We may expect the performance of them (Luke 1:38, 45; II Pet. 3:13). We should plead them in prayer (Gen. 32:9, 12; I Chron. 17:23, 26; Isa. 43:26).

Intercessory Prayer.

Closely linked with the promises of God is the child evangelist's resource of intercessory prayer. The two go together. Even the winning of a child in his days of innocence cannot be done without prayer. It is prayer that lays hold on God and calls down His power. It is through prayer that miracles are worked and hearts and minds are changed.

Intercessory prayer is commanded (I Tim. 2:1; Jas. 5:14, 16). It should be offered for children (Gen. 17:18; Matt. 15:22). It is sin to neglect it (I Sam. 12:23). God hears (Pss. 10:17; 65:2). God answers (Ps. 99:6; Isa. 58:9). Plead the promises of God when you pray (Gen. 32:9-12; Exod. 32:13; I Kings 8:26; Ps. 119:49). Ask in faith (Matt. 21:22; Jas. 5:15). Pray in the light of God's will (I John 5:14). Pray in the Name of Christ (John 14:13).

By this means, which God has put before us all, there is no saint who cannot go to prayer with the knowledge of God's will as found in the Word and claim the soul of any boy or girl to whom he is willing to go with the simple gospel message. God's Word is clear and plain.

The Will of God.

There is still another factor in our certain success as we give the gospel to the child. It is the expressed will of God. John tells us in I John 5:14-15, "If we ask any thing according to his will, he heareth us: and if we know that he hear us, whatsoever we ask, we know that we have the petitions that we desired of him." God has not left us in doubt as to His will in this matter. "Even so," said our Lord as He held the little child in His arms, "it is not the will of your Father which is in heaven, that one of these little ones should perish" (Matt. 18:14). We can go to

God in prayer on the behalf of any child to whom we are willing to witness and know that it is in accordance with His will. Knowing that it is His will, we know that He hears. Knowing that He hears, we know that we have the petition. What could be plainer or more certain?

If Matthew 18:14 were the only passage in all the Word of God that touched upon this matter, it would be enough; but there is much more in the Word. The Bible is full of exhortation to the people of God to impart a knowledge of God and His workings to the children. You will find the Old Testament again and again calling the fathers in Israel to make known the things of God to the children both in their homes and along the wayside. The New Testament presents an all-inclusive program of child evangelism for the age of grace.

Fathers are exhorted to bring up their children in the nurture and admonition of the Lord (Eph. 6:4). Parents should evangelize their own children. Leaders are commanded to feed the lambs (John 21:15). The workers of the church should seek to win every child that comes under the influence of the local congregation. But what of the boy or girl who has not the blessed privilege of hearing the gospel from the lips of his parents, who by virtue of distance or prejudice cannot be reached by the organized testimony of the church? What of him? Does not the Lord point us to such in Matthew 18:12-13 in the parable of the lost sheep? Individual believers should win the children of their neighborhoods, while they are children.

The Father's will, clearly set forth in the Word, is that the boys and girls be told the story of Jesus and His loving sacrifice. God stands ready to tell them through you. To the extent that you are willing to enter into it, His will is favorable to your successful ministry to the children.

CHILDHOOD—THE ACCEPTED TIME

Consider childhood itself as favorable to your purpose to evangelize the child. We have already learned that the child is trusting, sensitive, and teachable. These are factors that mean that your gospel ministry among them will be blessed with more fruit, all other things being equal, than among those of any other age group. That it will be real fruit and not merely apparent, if the evangelistic work is thorough, has already been demonstrated. There are still other qualities of childhood that stand you in good stead. The child has a hungry heart, an inquiring mind, and a mystic spirit.

Children are hungry for love. The loving atmosphere of the family circle is fast disappearing. The last few decades have witnessed the deterioration of the home from its high function as a place for loving, living and learning to a mere place of convenience. Consequently, the one thing that a child longs for more than anything else—love—is wanting in more than a few of today's homes. He wants attention and affection. He is starved for love. He is starved for you.

Another has said that the child first comes to love his teacher. Then he comes to love his teacher's Bible. The end is that he comes to love his teacher's Lord. It all begins with love. The child answers to love as he answers to nothing else. A little girl asked her Sunday School teacher, "Do you know why I love you?" "No. Tell me," was the teacher's response. "I guess it's because you love me." A week-day Bible club teacher, after her first attempt at gathering the boys and girls of her neighborhood into her home for a child-evangelism club, was startled to find almost the entire class returning evening after evening. She thought it was because she had failed in her explanation that the club was to meet but one afternoon a week. The real reason, however, came out in the words of the spokesman of the little group, who said, "We just want to come and be near you." Hungry hearts were answering to love.

The child has an inquiring mind. Virgin soil, this! He is thirsting for answers to the questions that swarm his mind. He wants to know; his questions come thick and fast when he finds someone who has his respect. The child must have certainty, especially in spiritual things. His keen mind goes to the very core of troublesome doctrines and less than satisfying truths. He is receptive. The doubtings of more mature years have yet to make their inroads and erect barriers to his knowing for himself the truths of God's Word.

It is this quality of childhood that makes children linger on and on, asking questions without end, at the close of a particularly helpful Bible lesson. All that they learn, in these years, must come from someone older. They are accustomed to listening that they might learn. They will listen to you and your message of certainty in eternal things just as readily as they listen to anyone else. Apart from earlier and heretical teaching, there is nothing that stands in the way of their absorbing the truth you give to them even as thirsty sand drinks up water.

The child is a mystic spirit. Using the word "religious" in its natural sense, someone once observed that a ten-year-old is the most religious person there is. Whether this is true or not may be questioned. At least we know that the older one grows the less inclined he is to mystic things except in times of stress and strain. The child lives very close to the border between the natural and the supernatural. Witness the fascination which fairy stories have for the young child. And for something a bit more fantastic, consider the so-called comic books with their unbelievable supermen whose superhuman deeds are so avidly followed by the young.

But taking the mystic quality of childhood in its better sense, and without reference to its abuse, there is no place in it for that crass materialism which prevents many an adult's receiving supernatural things. The child does not question the reality of the miracles of the Bible. The grand miracle of the resurrection is wholly reasonable; he does not think of questioning it. This is not a childish trait, but a childhood trait. But let the child grow up without faith in Christ and barren skepticism will take its place.

Childhood is the accepted time; it is the day of salvation, in a very real sense. Childhood itself is one of the greatest factors in the success of the children's worker. These truths were presented, along with the exhortation to ask boys and girls to accept Christ, to a group of Sunday School teachers. At the close of the session one of the group came to the front to say that she was going to her Sunday School class on Sunday with the intention of presenting the gospel fully and faithfully together with an invitation to her group of girls to receive the Lord then and there. A week later she returned, effervescent with joy, and yet with sorrow. To her surprise all fourteen of the girls in her class had openly received and confessed Christ. "And to think," she said, with tears glistening in her eyes, "that I've been teaching children for twenty years not knowing how natural it is for a youngster to respond to the gospel."

HELPS FOR YOUR SUCCESS

The body of helpful literature for the children's worker is substantial. There is hardly an evangelical publishing house that does not offer books and booklets related directly to the field of child evangelism. To the many books available must be added the Sunday School quarterlies with their faithful presentation of the gospel in all its applications.

Many visual aids are now available for your use. Pioneered by the Child Evangelism Fellowship, the visual method embodied in the flannelboard is now being used universally. This is a method of teaching designed for the beginner as well as for the experienced worker. It tends to hold the eye, that you might have the ear of the student as well.

A PRESENT OPPORTUNITY

Oh, the ubiquitous child! He is everywhere. His very presence spells success for you. Reachable? Show him the least bit of loving attention and he will swarm your doorstep. Many of these reachable, teachable, hungry little ones have never heard that God sent His Son to die in their stead and rise again that they might be made the children of God through faith in His Name. What an opportunity! It should stir you to win the children of your family connections. It should arouse you to a faithful evangelistic ministry in the Sunday School where there are never enough teachers at best. It should impel you to win the youngsters of your neighborhood through weekday Bible clubs, and whatever other agency you may discover.

Children can be won to Christ, and in the providence of God He has provided for your success in winning them.

Chapter III.

LEADING THE CHILD TO CHRIST

Children may be led to accept Christ during the course of a public meeting or through private dealing. In actual practice the child evangelist discovers that public presentation and private personal work are necessary. To present the complete picture of winning the child to a definite conversion, the course of this chapter will take you through the public ministry of the gospel into the more intimate and leisurely after-meeting. There will be the presentation of the Wordless Book story, followed by some methods of giving the invitation, and completed with instructions in dealing privately and intimately with those who respond.

THE WORDLESS BOOK

No gospel object has been marked with such success as an aid to giving the gospel as the Wordless Book. It is a small booklet, usually having a green cover, and pages of various colors. Each color speaks of some aspect of gospel truth. The cover page is page 1, pages 2 and 3 are black; pages 4 and 5 are red; pages 6 and 7 are white; and pages 8 and 9 are gold; so that as the pages are turned, a single color is presented to view.

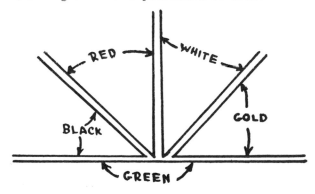

Wordless Books may be purchased at almost any Sunday School supply house or child evangelism supply depot. You can easily make one for yourself by purchasing the necessary colored paper from an artists' supply store and pasting the folded pages together according to the diagram above. A Wordless Book of a size that will conveniently fit into a brief case is an indispensable piece of soul-winning equipment.

Variations of the Wordless Book idea appear in the gospel walnut and the gospel blocks. The blocks, which have blue as an additional color, may be purchased. The gospel walnut may be made by sewing into a single strip small lengths of green, black, red, white and gold ribbon, in this order. Roll the finished strip into a small roll and insert into a hollowed-out English walnut shell held together with a rubber band. By drawing the ribbon out a color at a time, the gospel walnut enables the user to visualize the gospel step by step.

The Wordless Book is ideal for open-air work with casual groups. It arouses curiosity by its very nature. Workers who show its bright-green cover to playing children with the accompanying question, "Would you like to hear the story of this wordless book?" find an immediately interested audience. In larger sizes it may be used with great success from the platform.

For best results it is best to start with the gold page, although the object was designed with the thought of beginning with the black page and the facts a out sin. It was so used for years, but with no outstanding results. Then someone began to present the gold page first with the message of heaven, glory, and love. The results were phenomenal. The writer has seldom found it necessary to use more than the four colors already referred to—gold, black, red, and white. The green cover, which may speak of eternal life and growing in grace, may be used for the purpose of presenting assurance and instruction in the Christian life; but by the time that is in order, an open Bible has superseded the Wordless Book so that the object is neither necessary nor convenient.

Now to our public ministry of the gospel using this attention-getting and attention-holding visual aid. You have a small group of boys and girls around you in the open air. Or, the preliminaries are over in an indoor meeting, and you are ready to get down to cases with them. Here is the story of the Wordless Book in its essentials. It can be expanded with suitable illustrations, or its various points more fully developed according to the needs of the occasion. But in the main lines of treatment your story will take the following form:

YOU CAN TELL THIS STORY OF THE WORDLESS BOOK

Do you boys and girls like stories? Would you like to have me tell you a story? Do you like story books with pictures? My story book doesn't have a single picture in it. Perhaps you like the kind of story book that you have to read. Do you? Well, my story book doesn't have any words at all! That's why I call it my "Wordless Book." It hasn't any words; but its colored pages tell a story, the story of the Bible. Wouldn't you like to hear it?

When you read a story book do you begin here at the front? I don't. I begin at the back. Do you know why? I want to see if the story comes out all right, and if it does, then I begin to read from the beginning. My Wordless Book story has a lovely ending. It ends in heaven!

The Gold Page.
This gold page stands for heaven. Do you know, boys and girls, that God loves you so much that He wants you to be in heaven to enjoy it with Him forever? I can't begin to tell you how beautiful heaven is, but there is a verse in God's Word that gives us a hint. It is Revelation 21:21— "And the street of the city was pure gold." Let's say that together: "And the street of the city was pure gold." No one ever gets sick in heaven, no one ever has the least bit

of pain, or suffering, or sorrow. And what's better—no one ever dies. Revelation 21:4—"And God shall wipe away all tears from their eyes; and there shall be no more death, neither sorrow, nor crying, neither shall there be any more pain: for the former things are passed away."

No one but God could make such a wonderful place, and that is one reason why the Lord Jesus went back to heaven after He had come into the world and had lived and died and had risen from the dead. He went away to prepare a wonderful place for us (John 14:1-3). And the wonderful thing about it all is this, that God loves you so much that He wants you to be there with Him and to be perfectly happy forever and ever.

The Black Page.

If the street in front of your house were to be paved with pure gold, how long would it remain? Overnight? Why wouldn't it be there very long? Oh, someone would steal it! Is stealing a sin? Yes, it is. Boys and girls, no one will ever steal a single bit of the gold of the street of heaven, for God says, "There shall in no wise enter into it any thing that defileth, neither whatsoever worketh abomination, or maketh a lie" (Rev. 21:27). That means that no sin of any kind can ever enter heaven—not any at all! No stealing, no lying, no evil thing at all, will ever be allowed to spoil heaven.

You see, boys and girls, although God wants every one of us to be in heaven with Him, if there is sin in our hearts, that sin will keep us out of heaven.

This black page stands for sin, that ugly, terrible thing that will never be permitted to enter heaven. The Word of God tells us that "all have sinned, and come short of the glory of God" (Rom. 3:23). How many have sinned? All. Do you know anybody who has sinned? Who? You? Is it a sin to tell a lie? I wonder if there is any boy or girl here today who has never, never, never told an untruth? God says, "all have sinned." We too must say, "I have sinned," mustn't we?

Isn't that terrible? God loves us so much that He wants us to enjoy heaven with Him, but no sin can ever enter there, and we have sinned.

But listen, God has good news for us! He has made it possible for us to have our sins taken away! We can't take them away ourselves, can we? But He can, and He will— if we believe the gospel. That's good news, indeed, isn't it? That's exactly what the word "gospel" means—good news. And this is the gospel: "How that Christ died for our sins according to the scriptures; and that he was buried, and that he rose again the third day according to the scriptures" (I Cor. 15:3-4).

The Red Page.

You see, boys and girls, "all we like sheep have gone astray; we have turned every one to his own way; and the Lord hath laid on him the iniquity of us all" (Isa. 53:6). This red page stands for the blood of the Lord Jesus Christ. God tells us in His Word that "the blood of Jesus Christ his Son cleanseth us from all sin" (I John 1:7). God not only loved you so much as to want you to be in heaven with Him, but He loved you so much that He gave the Lord Jesus Christ, His only-begotten Son, to be your Saviour, to suffer and die in your place that your sins might be washed away.

He didn't need to die, for He was God. He said, "I lay down my life, that I might take it again. No man taketh it from me, but I lay it down of myself" (John 10:17-18). He wanted to take the punishment for our sins that we would not have to. When the Lord Jesus died on the cross, God put our sins upon Him. He died for us, in our place, for our sins. "He hath made him to be sin for us, who knew no sin; that we might be made the righteousness of God in him" (II Cor. 5:21). The Lord Jesus bore our sins in His own body on the cross (I Pet. 2:24).

And then, after He had died for our sins, according to the Scriptures, and after He had been buried, He arose from the dead! He is alive again! He lives! And because He lives, He is able to come into our hearts and live there.

After He had risen from the dead He said, "Behold, I stand at the door, and knock: if any man (or any boy or girl) hear my voice, and open the door, I will come in to him" (Rev. 3:20). When we invite Him to come into our hearts to live there as Saviour from sin, He does come in.

The White Page.

"For God so loved the world, that he gave his only begotten Son, that whosoever believeth in him should not perish, but have everlasting life" (John 3:16). The moment that we believe on the Lord Jesus Christ—and that means to open the doors of our hearts and receive Him into our hearts as our very own Saviour from sin—that moment He takes every sin away.

This white page stands for the hearts that are washed white when He comes in. Do you know how white He makes our hearts when we believe in Him? As white as snow? No! Whiter than snow! The Bible says, "Wash me, and I shall be whiter than snow" (Ps. 51:7). Wouldn't you like to have your heart washed that white? God wants you to have that kind of heart, and He is ready to make yours white the moment you receive the Lord Jesus as your Saviour.

You see, boys and girls, the Lord Jesus has taken the punishment for your sins, He has been made sin for you, He has borne your sins in His own body on the tree. He has done everything that He can do. Now, He wants to come into your heart and wash it clean and give you eternal life, life in heaven. He is knocking at your heart's door, and He wants you to open the door and let Him come in. He says: "I will come in." Wouldn't you like to have Him come into your heart today and live there forever, as the One who died for you and rose again? He will, if you will let Him.

Bow your head right now and ask the Lord Jesus to come into your heart and wash it whiter than snow. The Lord Jesus is God's gift to you. "For God so loved the world, that he gave his only begotten Son." You must receive Him if He is to be your Saviour.

And what do we do when we receive a gift? We say "Thank you," don't we? While our heads are still bowed and our eyes closed, if you have now received the Lord Jesus, then you just say, "Thank You" to God right now. Thank Him for heaven, for sending the Lord Jesus to die for you; thank Him for saving you and washing your heart whiter than snow. Thank Him for giving you eternal life.

Let me read a verse from God's Word. It is John 3:36: "He that believeth on the Son hath everlasting life." Have you believed on the Lord Jesus? Then, this verse is for you, isn't it? What does it say that you have? That's right—eternal life, the kind of life we must have for heaven. Aren't you glad that you have believed on the Lord Jesus Christ?

When we receive a gift we like to show that we appreciate it, don't we? The Lord Jesus says in John 14:15, "If ye love me, keep my commandments." We love the Lord Jesus now because He died for us, and He wants us to show our love by doing the things that will please Him. Where do we find what He would have us do? That's right—in the Bible.

There are many things He wants us to do. But there are two that we can begin to do today. One is to read His Word, the Bible (II Tim. 2:15). The other is to pray. "Pray without ceasing" (I Thess. 5:17). Every day, read the Bible. (Give a Gospel of John, if convenient.) It is food for saved boys and girls, and as we read it, we learn more and more about the Lord Jesus. Every day pray; and whenever you have troubles or problems, talk to the Lord Jesus about them.

Suppose we sin after we have believed on the Lord Jesus Christ? Here is what He wants us to do. I John 1:9: "If we confess our sins, he is faithful and just to forgive us our sins, and to cleanse us from all unrighteousness." He wants us to tell Him how we have sinned, and He promises to forgive us. We don't want to sin, and He doesn't want us to, but if we do, He cleanses us when we tell Him about it.

This story, as told above, is self-contained. The invitation is in it, with subsequent confirmation in the faith, and essential instruction in the first few steps in Christian living. We could conceivably let the matter rest here. Indeed, there are many occasions when circumstances will permit no further work with the children. Particularly is this true in open-air work. In public meetings, too, a child will respond to the invitation contained in the story. He will hold up his hand. But in the after-service, where more careful personal work is possible, he is absent for one reason or another. It is wise, therefore, to invite those youngsters who have responded, together with any others who did not respond but who are interested, to meet with you at the close of the service. There are several ways to do this, as we shall see.

THE INVITATION

There is a widespread fear of a mass movement of children in response to an open invitation. That fear is expressed again and again, but chiefly among those who have not witnessed a sane, carefully-planned and tactfully-executed public invitation. The writer has never seen a mass movement of children, such as that which is feared, at such a time! This is not to say that they do not occur. Undoubtedly they do, else we should not hear of them. Nor is this to say that he has not seen every child of an audience respond. That has been a blessed sight on several occasions, but in each such response it has been a thoughtful, prayerful, one-by-one, individual response whose sum was complete by the time the decision time came to an end.

The purpose of the invitation is to segregate those in whom conviction or faith has been wrought, that careful personal work may make sure the individual child has had a real heart experience of regeneration through faith in Christ. The child may have accepted Christ in the course of your message. That would be the ideal. On the other hand, he may have been convicted, but because of some unanswered question that has been raised in his mind, or because of some other barrier to faith, he has not received Christ, though he desires to do so. In either event, the invitation should be given that he may be separated for the purpose of meeting his individual need. You see, the response to the public invitation is not the end, but the means to the end.

The great danger in public invitations is that they are given, a response is had, noses are counted, and that is that! It should not be. So often the child who responds has made a decision. He has decided to accept Christ. But deciding to accept Christ and actually receiving Him are not necessarily one. To end the matter with the end of the invitation is to leave such a child with a good decision, but no knowledge of the way to execute it. As a matter of fact, this has been the curse of all public invitations that go no further, whether children or adults are involved. Every person, child or adult, who responds publicly to the gospel call should be led step by step through the gospel facts once again, and individually led to an acceptance of Christ or an affirmation that he has truly believed in Him earlier.

There are three things involved in the act of the will that appropriates Christ as Saviour:

Considering. Attention is fixed on one alternative; it is dismissed, and attention is turned to another. Many times such deliberation leads to the giving up of the idea and in not doing the thing. The period of deliberation, or "thinking it over," sometimes is a long one. It is a time of argument, the matter being looked at from all sides.

Deciding. The debate must come to an end and a decision made. After the prodigal son had debated his condition, he said, "I will arise and go to my father." Decision ends deliberation and requires an effort of the will. To "make up our minds" is not always easy. Because it links decision with an act, the raising of the hand, or some similar gesture of decision, is good applied psychology.

Acting. The third thing is to do the thing decided upon. Many a good decision is never carried out. The secret of carrying out a decision of the will is to find the way or the plan by which to carry it out. You as a teacher must often suggest to your pupils the plan for carrying out their decisions.

What Sort of Public Invitation Shall We Give?

The writer sometimes does this. The message is ended. Hands have been raised. Prayer has been offered. The end of the service is at hand. Perhaps a closing song is about to be sung and the group dismissed. The invitation takes this form: "I'd like to talk with the boys and girls who have believed on the Lord Jesus Christ today. We are going to sing another song and then the meeting will be dismissed. If you have believed on the Lord Jesus, or if you would like to but don't know just how to do it, you come down here while the other boys and girls are going out of the room, and we'll have a little talk about the Lord Jesus Christ and about becoming a Christian." Then the closing song is sung, the final prayer offered, and the group dismissed. It has never ceased to be a miracle to the writer that in the hustle and bustle and rush to get out into the open again that so much as a single child should remain behind. Surely they won't. But they do! Some will linger along, moving down slowly and by a circuitous route. Some will come directly. Some will come noisily. Some will come quietly and with embarrassment. But they will come. Then they are dealt with, either in a group with individual confessions of faith drawn from them, or, if helpers are available, they are dealt with in the group on the basis of the gospel, usually using the Wordless Book again briefly, following which they are divided into smaller groups for individual questioning and help.

Another method of giving a public invitation is to have the boys and girls bow their heads and close their eyes. Briefly, the essentials are gone over again, and a show of hands is asked for after this fashion: "Let every head be bowed, every eye closed. No one is to look up. Fold your hands. Now, is there a boy or girl here who never before today has accepted the Lord Jesus Christ as his Saviour?

And now you want to receive Him into your heart today. If you do, or if you've already received Him today, just hold up your hand so that I may know who you are. Is there one? Is there one boy or girl who will lift his hand and let me know that he wants to receive the Lord Jesus Christ?" (It is best to say, "Is there one?" Keep it individual. Take no note of those who hold up their hands. Boys and girls will be seen raising them several times, higher and higher! So far as they are concerned there are no others involved in the invitation.)

Wait for the hands. Give time for the child to decide. Watch carefully and you will see hesitation, indecision, finally victorious faith, revealed in the raising of the hand. The hand will start up and be quickly withdrawn. Again the youngster will start to raise his hand, but the enemy is at work and the hand is brought down. And then, vigorously and victoriously it will go up, fully extended!

While heads are still bowed, lead in prayer asking the Christian boys and girls to pray silently. With heads still bowed, ask the boys and girls who have raised their hands to move out of their seats and come to the front of the room. Let the others know that if they did not hold up their hands, but would likewise like to receive the Saviour, that they may come too, for you want to talk to them about the Lord and about being a Christian. This may take a bit of waiting and a repetition or two of what it is that you want them to do. Give plenty of time. Then with the group before you, go over the Wordless Book again briefly and either send the entire group to an inquiry room, or dismiss the audience and carry on the after-meeting right there.

It is the spirit of individual decision and the atmosphere of prayer that prevents a thoughtless mass movement.

AFTER THE INVITATION—WHAT?

Since the purpose of the public invitation is to afford an opportunity to work with each youngster individually, we want to be sure that we employ the opportunity. Here are some pointers to help in the after-meeting or in the inquiry room. It is assumed that much of the work of evangelizing them has already been accomplished and the youngsters have indicated some degree of willingness to be saved. These instructions likewise cover the more leisurely matter of leading a child to Christ during the course of a private and intimate conversation, perhaps upon his asking a question pertaining to spiritual things.

1. Be Sure to Use Your Open Bible.

Open it and keep it opened. Read, rather than quote, from its pages. The c h i l d must understand that this is God's Word to him, not your thoughts or reasonings. Only thus can you cope with some questions which may arise concerning many conflicting teachings with which the child may have had contact.

Have the child read, if he can do so. If he does not read readily, or if there are several youngsters before you, have each in turn put his finger on the passage you have read.

It is wise to keep to a few passages. Too many tend to confuse the child and render almost impossible the making of each point crystal clear. Use but one, or at the most two, passages on each point, and take the time to drive each one home.

A device which the writer often uses is to have all repeat significant phrases with him after he has read the passage as a whole. He then follows with leading questions which are designed to impress their significance upon the youngsters.

2. Be Sure Your Explanation of the Gospel is Clear.

I Corinthians 15:3-4 is your basic passage. This is the Word's own definition of the gospel. Use it. Read the passage, giving the meaning. Let your treatment be as full as the needs of the child require. If there is any doubt that he has not been sufficiently evangelized, go over the ground again. Begin with the love of God and heaven (Rev. 21:4, 21, 27; John 3:16). Go on to develop the fact of sin which you have touched on in Revelation 21:27 using Romans 3:23. Then present the gospel facts of I Corinthians 15:3-4—Christ's death for our sins, His burial, His resurrection. Stress the fact that this gospel is the power of God unto salvation to those who believe it (Rom. 1:16).

Give these five steps on fingers, having the child repeat them:

1. God loved
2. I sinned
3. Christ died
4. I believe
5. I live

3. Be Sure the Holy Spirit is Working.

This is not our work; it is the Spirit's. Watch for the evidence that He is at work. Wait, if necessary. He alone can convict of sin, of the need of a Saviour. It is only He who can reveal Christ as Saviour, even to a child.

Do not force the decision. Be tender. Remember that you are an adult while the one before you is a child. Living as he does in what seems to be an adult world, he is only too quick to render the outward appearance of acceding to what he believes is your desire. As you progress in your dealing, the Holy Spirit will use the Word which you give to work conviction.

Watch those eyes! They are the mirror of the soul. You will see in them the child's concern, his conviction of sin, his awakened hope, his joy as he receives the Lord. Those eyes will tell you when to go on to the next step—watch them!

4. Be Sure You Take Nothing for Granted.

Ask questions. Ask them at every turn. Phrase your questions so that the correct answer is apparent. Put them bluntly when you sense the need of testing the child's grasp of any particular phase of the truth you are presenting. Pause in your reading of proof-texts to ask questions that will both test their comprehension and confirm the truth to them.

Here are some passages you will probably use, together with questions you might need to ask:

Romans 3:23. How many have sinned? Does that mean all of us? Does it mean you? Is it a sin to tell a lie? Can you take back a single sin?

Isaiah 53:6. What has God done with our sins?

I Corinthians 15:3-4. For whose sins did Christ die? Did He die for your sins?

I Peter 2:24. What did He do with our sins? Was He bearing your sins?

Revelation 3:20. Will the Lord Jesus come into our hearts if we let Him? Will you let Him come in by saying, "Come into my heart, Lord Jesus"? Did He promise to come in? Did you invite Him in? Then, did He come in? Will you put your finger on the verse where He makes the promise?

Other questions will suggest themselves as you use various passages, and as the occasion demands.

As you ask the questions, make it known that you expect answers. Simple nods of the head are not always sufficient. Verbal answers are best. You may have to ask the question several times, or perhaps rephrase it, before the first answer comes. Usually, however, once the ice is broken, the answers will come. With the first embarrassed answer there comes complete freedom to respond to further questions, and as self-consciousness disappears his answers will come readily with his comprehension.

5. Be Sure You Keep to the Single Issue of Receiving Christ.

As often as needful, emphasize the fact that salvation comes through believing a message from God—the gospel —and through receiving a Person—the Lord Jesus Christ. Don't confound this issue with anything else, however needful in its place. The Lord has a way of working things out in His own orderly fashion. Your objective is to open the heart of the youngster before you. Through that opened door you expect him to admit the Lord Jesus to live within as his own Saviour forever. Keep to that single objective.

A favorite passage, which the writer uses almost exclusively in this connection, is Revelation 3:20. It is a transaction that the child can understand, though there may be perplexities to be cleared away. A five-year-old upon hearing this verse said, "But how can I open the door?" I likened it to someone knocking for admission to our home and briefly explained that we must give the Lord permission to enter. Immediately she responded, "Oh, I know! He won't come in unless we let Him come in." Quickly she bowed her head and in a childish prayer received Him into her own heart.

What Next?

The work of leading a child to Christ is initial only. The task is not done, it is only begun. There is a life of faith to be lived in the Holy Spirit. There is to be growth in grace and in the knowledge of the Lord and Saviour Jesus Christ. There is a life of service through the power of the Holy Spirit to be rendered in and through the church of Jesus Christ. Often the fuller instructions must be left to other hands. In any case, it must be left with the one Teacher, and we must follow each child in confident prayer that what God has begun in his life He will perform until the day of Jesus Christ (Phil. 1:6).

In no event should you leave the child without first giving him the assurance of salvation from the Word. Such passages as John 1:12 or John 5:24 may be used. Then give the child instruction in those things which he may begin to do that same day: 1. Read a portion of the Word daily. 2. Pray at every opportunity and at regular times. 3. Confess Christ as Saviour with the mouth. Use the question method here, and present these things from the pages of your Bible.

Chapter IV.

THE TEACHER'S TASK

The teacher's task is not an easy one nor a light one. The issues are heaven and hell. The opposition is satanic. Fallen human nature, even in a child, is wholly depraved. Teaching the Word of God to boys and girls demands the best that you can give. It means diligent application to the task at hand. It calls for studied preparation. It requires constant prayer, unceasing devotion, wholehearted attention to every detail.

A poor idea of Bible teaching is that the teacher simply passes on to the pupil some information which he did not possess before. Teaching is much more than that. God would make truth plain through people. Your personality must make the truth you teach a living thing. The class must feel the power of your personality in the truth you teach. Your constant aim must be to combine the truth taught to the pupil with a Christian example lived before him. The truth must come through you and not merely through your lips.

"Take heed unto thyself, and unto the doctrine (thy teaching); continue in them: for in doing this thou shalt both save thyself, and them that hear thee" (I Tim. 4:16).

The Teacher

The teacher must be a born-again Christian. If you do not know the way, how can you lead others? If you have not had a heart experience of Christ in salvation, how can you expect to do His work? Can the blind lead the blind? "Ye must be born again" (John 3:7). This is the foundation upon which the teacher must stand.

The teacher must have a definite purpose in teaching. That purpose must be the right one. There is no place among the Lord's harvest-workers for the personally ambitious. If desire for place and prominence supplies the motive for your work, you are on the wrong course. Teaching the Word of God calls for a careful examination of purposes and motives.

The teacher must appreciate the sacredness of the trust that is committed to him, and the tremendous responsibility of handling the Word of God when the souls of boys and girls are at stake. It is serious business!

The teacher must be willing to prepare consecratedly and painstakingly. The effort called for is not a little, but the reward is great. Slipshod preparation, when eternity is in view and the souls of boys and girls are in your care, is devilish.

The Teacher's Method

What are we to teach? A lesson? More than that. The little boy who, when asked if he had learned about Jesus in his class, replied that he hadn't—that was at the other end of the book—indicated the whole company of teachers who are given to the mere teaching of a lesson.

Our teaching is the teaching of the cross. It is central. It is fundamental. All else stems from the transaction of Calvary. Every lesson, therefore, should point to the cross. The gospel should be given in every lesson. It need not occupy the whole, but it should occupy some part. Every child should have the opportunity to hear the story of redemption, even though in brief, at every session. Beyond that, an opportunity should be afforded him to receive the Christ who died for him.

Beyond the cross is the empty tomb. The two are inseparably linked. There is hardly a class, at least among those who are reaching new boys and girls from time to time, that will not have in it two needy groups—those who have not yet been saved, and those who have. Each group has its particular need, whether it be Christ as Saviour, or Christ as Lord. This must be kept in mind at all times.

The problem is to teach in such a manner that the needs of each may be met.

Since it is true that the larger teaching ministry of the Holy Spirit cannot become effectual for the individual until that one has become the residence of the Spirit through a new birth, conversion must come first. You must evangelize to teach. Evangelize first; then your teaching of the Word may result in the child's receiving the things of the Spirit of God, and he may "grow in grace and in the knowledge of our Lord and Saviour Jesus Christ" (II Pet. 3:18). But it is still true that "the natural man receiveth not the things of the Spirit of God: for they are foolishness unto him: neither can he know them, because they are spiritually discerned" (I Cor. 2:14).

In every lesson, then, two elements must be blended in such proportions as the composition of your class shall require. You must provide for the youngster who has not yet been saved. He needs to have the way of salvation clearly, although it may be briefly, explained. This can be done. No printed sermon of Spurgeon's fails to do it, even in messages directed to the saved. Then, there is the youngster who has received Christ. His needs are vastly different. He has already received a new life in Christ, but he must be developed in his Christian walk.

Your responsibility is to meet the heart need of every boy and girl who is before you as you minister the Word of God. It will be necessary for you to learn as much as you can about the individual boys and girls before you, if you are to satisfy their needs. Meet them on that level. Build each up from that level, remembering that "other foundation can no man lay than that is laid, which is Jesus Christ" (I Cor. 3:11). Your aim must be to bring boys and girls to Him and then to build them up in Him. This you can do for your group as a whole only as you do it for the individual.

The Teacher's Purpose
The successful teacher of boys and girls will seek to accomplish three very essential things in every lesson.

First, he will attempt to communicate Bible knowledge in such a way that the mental powers of each pupil will seize upon it and assimilate it.

Next, he will illustrate and apply the knowledge thus imparted in such fashion as to arouse the emotions, that the pupil may feel that he should do or be what he should do or be in the light of his newly acquired knowledge. Do not be alarmed at the phrase "arouse the emotions." This is a very essential operation of the mind, as we shall soon see.

Finally, the teacher will encourage the pupil to do the thing that he feels he ought to do.

Reaching the Will.

NEVER FORGET THIS: The operations of the mind may be summed up under three heads—(1) KNOWING, (2) FEELING, (3) WILLING.

KNOWING includes such powers of the mind as memory, imagination, deliberation, judgment and reasoning.

FEELING, or emotion, includes those states of mind which give pleasure or pain, such as love, hatred, anger, jealousy, joy, grief, shame.

WILLING includes the mental states leading to action, such as impulse, decision, doing.

Whenever you teach the Word effectively, these three operations of the mind are exercised by your pupil—and always in that order. For instance, you present the gospel message and your pupil hears it intelligently (knowing). You illustrate and apply the truth until your pupil realizes that he is not saved but desires to be (feeling). He decides to receive Christ as his Saviour and does so (willing).

As a teacher you must take the first two steps in the process before you can hope to storm the citadel of your pupil's will. All too many have the mistaken idea that to present the facts and to call for action should bring about the pupil's decision. But it is not so. The second step must be taken.

The Power Behind the Will—Feeling.

Do not be unduly alarmed about this matter of arousing the pupil's feelings—the will is never exercised without the stimulus coming through the kindled emotions. That is the way the Lord has constituted mankind. No one acts upon knowledge apart unfeelingly, not even those who are overwhelmingly intellectual. The order always has been, is now, and always will be this, as the will moves to action: We know clearly; we feel keenly; we act promptly. Truth stirs the feelings; the feelings stir the will; the will produces action. Action is what we seek.

Why is it that the feelings move the will? It is this: When the feelings are aroused by a truth, a deep impression is made. Such an impression always seeks expression in some way. The deeper the impression that is made, the keener will be the emotion felt, and the more urgent will be the desire for an outlet of expression. A man who is violently angry may, in his anger, destroy things. A child may throw himself to the floor, kicking and screaming. The expressions may differ, but the course is the same in all cases.

Feeling, you see, is a powerhouse whose fuel is information. Don't attempt to go from the fuel pile of knowledge to the high-tension lines of action without going through the powerhouse of emotion. It can't be done.

This is true of all minds, whether of children or adults. There is no difference. All operate in exactly the same way. Do not, therefore, fear aroused emotion in your pupil. Rather, seek to arouse it through the right kind of knowledge—the facts of the Word of God.

Three Steps

To sum up, then: You must first arouse the pupil's mind and direct it to the facts you wish to drive home. The pupil must grasp the facts that you present. He must receive them. Then you must illustrate and apply the facts to the point where his emotions are called into play and he feels that he should take the action called for. Finally, this blending of knowledge and feeling must be fanned into flame as conviction takes hold and the pupil's will is exercised in his decision: "I will do this; I will be this."

The will is what we are after—to bend it to Christ. The purpose is good; be sure that your procedure is right. Just as no two fingerprints are alike, so no two minds are the same. But the main avenues to the will are the same in all. In some, it will be found true that a little knowledge plus a great deal of feeling will move to action. In others, much knowledge with little feeling leads to the same end. And in between, are many gradations.

But the steps are always the same: KNOWING, FEELING, WILLING.

THE STORY IS THE THING

No teaching vehicle affords such an opportunity to reach the will of the child through his feelings as does a well-told story. It is the ideal teaching method. Our Lord used it again and again with telling effect on His hearers. So should we.

The reason for the effectiveness of the story is that it calls for the exercising of the pupil's imagination. If knowledge is the fuel which runs the powerhouse of feeling, imagination is surely the kindling which starts the fire. Imagination stirs the feelings and, we have already learned, this is the immediate approach to the will.

The Story's Value.

When truths are made to live, they become real. Imagination strengthens the memory, so that when we once see a truth with the "mind's eye," it is firmly fixed. Why do we remember childhood stories? Because imagination once made them real. We lived them, and they became vitally a part of our body of experience.

In the story method of teaching, Bible characters are brought to life and may be observed as individuals. Their peculiarities, their weaknesses, their virtues—all may be displayed in such a way that the imagination of the child takes them up, clothes them with reality, and lives with them for the time. He walks with them and talks with them. In this way, Bible characters are a living influence upon the pupil.

The story teaches by indirection. The pupil, through the power of his own imagination, becomes identified with the chief character of the story. To all intents and purposes, he becomes the chief character. As the story unfolds, he feels whatever is represented as happening to the story's hero. He suffers with him; he rejoices with him; he struggles with him; he triumphs with him. For the time, the pupil is David gaining victory over Goliath; Moses at the burning bush; Paul on the Damascus road; or whoever the story's leading personage happens to be.

It is characteristic of childhood that facts and fancies should blend into each other. The child lives in "wonderland" all day long. For him, fancy changes boxes into castles, sticks into horses, stones into fruits and pastries. It is this native capacity of the child to exercise his imagination that makes possible his stepping over into the story to become the leading character in it.

Once again we state that the three steps which are taken as the mind learns are these: KNOWING, FEELING, WILLING. See how the story easily and naturally takes this course to action. It supplies the facts to be known. This it does in a most palatable way, bearing them along on a stream of story action. The child's mind grasps them as a matter of course and, because imagination is making them real, stores them away in memory's treasure house. The child becomes the leading character and feels what he feels. And, because for the time he is the hero, he wills what the hero wills.

The story, it can be seen, is the ideal teaching method. Use it.

The Illustrative Story.

There are two varieties of stories being used by teachers of boys and girls.

First, there is the story which illustrates Bible truth. As usually encountered, this is a story out of life which is interesting in itself and lends itself to a Biblical application at the close. A great many teachers use this type of story with some measure of success. It is not, however, the best kind. It fails to recognize the manner in which the mind operates.

Such a story occupies itself with stirring the feelings, but the information which generates feeling is not the Word of God, but the vehicle to which it is attached as a sort of trailer. Not until feelings have been aroused is the Bible application brought in. This is not the best order, and it is doubtful if the knowledge injected late in the story is really absorbed. It is also questionable whether the will can be effectively reached, since there is little consistency in the teaching pattern, following as it does such a course as this: secular or moral information; feeling; Biblical application; appeal to the will.

As an illustration embodied in a more direct approach through a pure Bible story, these "almost" Bible stories do have a definite place. They should not, however, be the chief offering.

The Bible Story.

There seems to be a widespread misconception that boys and girls must have their Biblical information well-diluted. It is on this account that the illustrative story just described has caught on with teachers of children. But there is a more excellent way.

Boys and girls do not need to have the milk of the Word watered down. They can receive it as it is.

The writer reasons that if it is the Word which God has designed to use in saving souls and building them up in Christ, then our messages and stories should be as Biblical in content as it is possible for us to make them. Let your stories be Bible stories, right from the text of God's Word. This is reasonable, for the pupil's mind is approached on the basis of Bible knowledge imparted; this knowledge, applied and illustrated, kindles the emotions and imagination grasps it; and the will, when it acts, does so consistently. The order is right—the results are certain.

Childhood's imagination is stirred by stories of real experiences. Children are hero worshipers, loving to hear of men and their deeds of bravery. Is it not wise, then, to use the very real, the absolutely true stories of the Bible? Fortunately, the Bible can be the most attractive of story books when properly handled. Let it be the source of your stories.

PREPARING A BIBLE STORY

We come now to the matter of studying and preparing your Bible story. If you would teach boys and girls effectively, expect to work at it. Your Bible story must be carefully and thoroughly studied—from the pages of the Word of God itself, if it is to be a profitable one. Do not be self-deceived in this matter. Nowhere does slipshod preparation produce its inevitable harvest of failure and disappointment so certainly as in the Bible story method of teaching. Your success or failure here is very largely determined by the quality and extent of your preparation.

Do not expect to tell an interesting story, driving home its message and sounding out its exhortations, without adequate study and planning. Casual, hit-or-miss reading over the text or scanning some predigested lesson leaflet will not suffice; your Bible story must be really studied. It must be the product of prayerful meditation, cautious treasure-mining, Spirit-taught seeking of the Bible's precious truths. There is no easy way—it is exacting work, demanding your best application to the task. The easy way is the way of failure, and we dare not fail when heaven and hell are the issues involved.

I. READ CAREFULLY.

There is no substitute for careful reading and rereading of all that the Bible has to say about the story for which you are studying. Take your Bible, and with paper and pencil at hand—if you are one of those who like to jot down fleeting ideas at once lest they be lost—read and read and read.

Read all the accounts, if there are several. Study the
cross-references. Do not be content with less than complete mastery of what the Scripture says. Why? Because
you can tell the story only as well as you know it.

There are three rules for profitable Bible study which
apply here. They are:

First, read your Bible.

Second, read your Bible.

Third, read your Bible.

For the Bible story, you must read purposefully. Your
reading prepares you for your presentation before a group
of boys and girls. There must be a system in your reading.
We give you a simple scheme of study which will be of
help to you. It will point out to you those things which
you will seek to discover, to be used in your story, as you
study the Word.

1. Read for the narrative.

First of all, you will read for the purpose of establishing
the narrative in your own mind. What is the story about?
What happens? Many times a single reading will reveal
the flow of events and their sequence; but more often two
or more passages must be put together and the narrative
pattern worked out from all the Scriptures relating to the
lesson. Read first to get the drift of the story so that you
may see its several events in their proper order and relationship.

2. Read to meet the characters.

Second, read for the purpose of becoming acquainted
with the persons involved in the story. Who are they?
What are they like? What can you find out about them
from other passages? A good Bible dictionary can be a
useful tool here; it will give you a digest of the career of
every person who is mentioned in the Scriptures. Study
each character until you know him, his life history, and
especially his part in the story you are studying.

It is necessary to know all that you can about your characters. Learn their peculiarities, their hopes and fears, their motives. Then, when you come to the telling of the story, you can present them to your boys and girls as living personages, not fictional puppets.

3. Read for the action and conflicts.

Your third reading should find you absorbing the action and conflicts. This is the dramatic skeleton without which your story will have no life or movement. Note every conflict. There are but three varieties: (1) Man against nature; (2) Man against other beings; (3) Man against self. And, of course, there is action, both in the conflict and after the conflict. It is this drama that will capture the attention and hold the interest while you drive home the Word to your listening pupils.

4. Read to divide into scenes.

You are now ready to read with a view to discovering the several scenes. How many are there? Who is present in each? What is going on? What is the particular conflict in each one? As you read, notice the shifting scenery, the coming and going of the various people of the story, the locations to which the action takes you. All this is important, for your story will take the form of a scene-by-scene dramatization, in a measure at least.

5. Read for movement and gestures.

The fifth time you go over the text, read with an eye to the gestures the characters are probably making. These would be the visible keys to their inward emotions. Watch the movement of the people. As you tell the story later, you will want to be several characters in turn, making the same gestures and movements.

As you read for these various purposes, you will find it profitable to let your imagination have free rein, for on many of these points no exact information will be given in the text itself. It will be necessary for you to imagine the action and the reactions of the characters, as well as much of the movement and gestures.

You will need background material if you are to place the action of your story in its proper setting. A Bible dictionary can be a great help in this. Whatever lesson helps, such as dictionaries, commentaries, quarterlies, etc., are available to you should be left strictly alone until you have first mastered the text itself by reading along some such lines as suggested above. Then you may turn to them with profit, and they become what they should be—"helps." But do not turn to them first; the Bible is to be your source, all else taking a secondary place.

Try this plan of reading, following it rigidly at first. Do not eliminate anything. Later you can take short cuts, but not at first. As you develop a "story bias," with your mind alert for story material, you will develop your own system and will build your story as you go along.

II. REVIEW SLOWLY.

After reading and reading again in studying for your Bible story, comes the review. Have you really mastered the text? Your review will tell you.

1. Read.

The first step in reviewing is to read the Scripture text, keeping in view the five things mentioned above: (1) the narrative; (2) the characters; (3) the action; (4) the scenes; (5) the gestures. In all this will be incorporated such background material as you have gathered from various sources.

This reading must be done slowly. Haste is waste here. Take time to ponder the story as you read. The point is not to attempt to memorize—but rather to "see" the story as if you were a firsthand witness.

2. Outline.

You are ready now to put on paper an outline summary of the story. This need not be too elaborate. Make it as brief as you can. The purpose is to open another "gate" to your own consciousness. So far you have been reading;

only the eye gate has been used. Now, in addition, you are
to do as well as see, thus strengthening the impression.
This is your "handwork." Your notes are not in order to
refresh your memory as you teach. Consign them to the
wastebasket as soon as they are made. They are made
in order to fix the story in your mind so that you will have
no need of them at the time of delivery.

Perhaps you will find it necessary to refer to your Bible
as you make your first notes. That's all right, do it. But
throw your notes away when they are completed and make
another set, from memory this time. The second set will
probably be more condensed. Good! You are really making
progress. If you would really profit by this exercise, keep
on until you can set down just a few key words which will
suggest to you the entire story.

But don't expect to use any notes when you teach. You
won't need them if you've come this far. More than that,
you will find that they slow you down too much as the
inspiration of an attentive group, listening with rapt interest, grips you.

3. Check

Now check yourself on each of the five points you have
been studying. Can you recite the narrative? At least
in skeleton outline? Who are the characters and what do
you know about each one? What are the conflicts? Go
through all the points, taking them one at a time, and test
yourself thoroughly. If you find that you are uncertain
about any one of them, go back over that ground again.
Don't rest until you have it. Your aim is to study so well
that you'll know all there is to know about what takes
place. You want to be sure about who does what; when
and where he does it; and who was looking on, or oppos-
ing him.

III. RECONSTRUCT IMAGINATIVELY.

Now for a bit of mental gymnastics which will pay rich
dividends. It is simple to sit down, comfortably relaxed,

and let your mind reconstruct the story. For the moment, let your mind be a screen upon which the changing scenes are projected. Watch them with the eye of your mind. Listen to the characters as they encounter each other. Let your attention focus upon everything—the scenic background, the dress, the everyday customs—everything. Put into the picture all that you have learned from your study and research.

This is not to be done with speed. Don't hasten it. Take the time to permit associations to form and lead you along uncharted paths. This is imaginative—and it is creative. Imagination is making it real. But more than that, while you are doing this, the story is becoming a part of you. You are living it as a matter of personal experience, just as you want the boys and girls to enter into it and live it as you reconstruct it for them audibly.

Now try this—go back over the story again. But this time imagine yourself stepping into the action and taking the part of each person in the story. Be that character as he is at the forefront. Try to think as he would think, feel as he would feel, do as he would do. Do it with each successive character as he comes to the front of the scene in the developing action. It may be difficult at first, but persevere; it is the key to successful dramatization of the story when you come to give it.

This is probably looming up before you as a great deal of effort for a single story. It is! But what we are giving you is for your first story. The second one you prepare will go more easily. And once you develop your own variation of the system we have been giving you, modified and adapted to your own particular needs, you will find it a much simpler undertaking. But always it will be work, hard work. The need for that will not cease.

But we are still not through with our preparation of the story. We must still plan our story in its approach, its presentation, and its conclusion. This we will consider next.

PLANNING THE BIBLE STORY

Before we go any further, suppose we look back at your preparation thus far.

Have you prepared yourself, as well as your story? Not only study of the text is called for, but meditation upon it and much prayer. You must think of the lesson in terms of your own experience as well as in the light of the needs of the boys and girls whom you teach.

Have you discovered a main thought, idea or principle which the lesson centers around? Your story should be a tool used to plant this one main thought and idea in the pupil's mind in such a way that he will be led to act upon it.

Have you prepared your pupils for the lesson? As much as possible, gain their confidence, their friendship, their personal regard, through personal contacts during the week. Have a personal acquaintance with each child. You must know them as individuals in all their peculiarities. Prepare each lesson in the light of your knowledge of your pupils.

So far, we have been occupied chiefly with acquiring a great familiarity with the materials for the story. No doubt by the time your study has progressed to this point, you will have some idea of the form your story will take, and, no doubt, your story plan has been formulated to a great extent. But let us look more closely at the three elements which go to make it up. They are: (1) the body of the story; (2) the application; (3) the approach.

I. THE BODY OF THE STORY.

Every truth in every lesson cannot be taught. You do not have the time. Some truths must be selected, others passed over. In the main, your selection will be based on two factors, the pupil's level of attainment and the main direction of the story itself.

Theme

Every Bible story must have a central theme running through it. It is this which supplies its direction. The narrative is the vehicle, the theme is the cargo. What is the theme of your story? Decide upon it. If it is not evident to you, go no further without settling upon it. Everything else will depend on this one thing. It is the heart of your message.

State your theme. In a single sentence, not too long, sum up the whole message your story is going to carry to your pupils. Your theme probably can be stated in a variety of ways. Here is where your knowledge of your pupils' development and needs comes in. State your theme in such a way that its direction is toward them.

Are you telling the story of Noah and the flood, and do your pupils need to accept Christ? Then your theme might be stated in this fashion: Only those who believe God and take His way may be saved. Perhaps you expect to tell the same story to a group of boys and girls who have never been evangelized—they know nothing at all of the gospel message. Your theme might take a longer form and be put this way: God will judge sin, but He provides a way of escape for those who will take it.

The theme, it can be seen, determines the direction which the story will take in its treatment and applications. In the first case just suggested, the story would feature the ark as a place of safety from the flood judgment and the Lord Jesus as today's place of safety, with the stress upon the necessity for believing and entering in, if either is to avail for the individual. In the second case, sin, God's holy hatred for iniquity, and His certain judgment would probably be emphasized first, with His gracious provision in the ark, and in Christ, completing the presentation.

Scenes

Having settled upon the theme which your story will have as its core, your next step is to divide the action into convenient scenes. Each scene must be a unit of action or conflict which carries the story along on its way to the climax. If your story is well balanced, the climax will come in the final scene when the theme is fully and dramatically proved.

There will, no doubt, be a need for either selection or invention, or both, at this point as the need of your theme may require. The complete Scriptural record may conceivably contain many incidents which make no contribution to the theme as you have stated it. Very well, do not use them. This is especially true when teaching chapter by chapter through a Book of the Bible.

It is easier to select than it is to invent. But invention is often called for. Take the case of Noah and the first theme stated above. The details given in the text are meager. God tells Noah to build the ark; Noah builds it, enters it, and the flood comes. It doesn't take long to give the details as they are found in the Word. Suppose we use our imagination and do a bit of inventing. Bring in Noah's unbelieving neighbors and let Noah preach to them. Let them taunt him when he enters the ark. Finally, have them come in terror, as the rains descend, and attempt to enter the closed door.

Your scenes will take definite shape as you do this, perhaps after the following fashion: First scene: God and Noah in conference; Second scene: Noah building the ark and preaching to his scoffing neighbors; Third scene: Noah and his company entering the ark as the ungodly taunt and deride him; Fourth scene: Noah safe in God's appointed place with the godless outside the closed door, their judgment at hand.

As you become more and more experienced in building your own story, you will discover that the story will naturally develop as you study and restudy in preparation. But always its development should be divided into well-defined scenes.

The body of your story must carry the load. It supplies the reality, which the mind of the child grasps, so that he KNOWS. Its action and conflict become a true emotional experience of his very own and its decisions become his as he FEELS and WILLS.

II. THE APPLICATION.

Truth must be applied if the child's will is to be reached. He must be stirred to feeling that he should be, or do, what is being taught, before he can be brought to take the necessary action. Applications are vital. This is the question: WHAT DO I WANT MY PUPILS TO DO AS A RESULT OF THIS LESSON?

There are two ways in which you may apply truth. You may make what we shall call a running application by applying truth as you have opportunity and occasion during the telling of the story proper. Or you may reserve your application until last, first telling the story for the story's sake, then going back over the high ground in a pointed way with a view to driving home the truth which the story carries.

The particular story, together with the particular situation, will usually govern the method employed; but it will be generally found possible to make the lesser applications as you tell the story, reserving the major one for that final, critical moment just after the climax of the story has been reached. Interest is held more easily all the way through when this is done.

For most of us it would be better if we attempted less, and took more time to associate new truth with truth already known. After all, it is in this way that the pupil adds to his store of knowledge—he links the new with the old. There is no other way for new truth to be learned. The teacher must find the level of the lass and start from that point.

Before you attempt to teach, answer these two questions: (1) What in my pupils' experience is like the truth in this lesson? (2) What stories, illustrations, comparisons, or word pictures will best throw light upon the new truths of the lesson? The story of the good Samaritan is the ideal example of how our Lord taught in this way. There are two steps which you must take: First, select as a starting point something seen or known by the pupils.

Second, go forward by means of comparisons from the known to the new or unknown truth.

The gospel facts should be clearly and emphatically stated in every lesson, and the unsaved should be told how they may be saved. This may have to be done briefly and quickly in many situations, but it must be done if you would be true to your great responsibility. Moreover, some opportunity should be afforded the child to act upon this gospel truth by receiving the Lord, even though it may of necessity be limited to the bowing of the head during a moment of quietness and decision just before the final prayer.

Make much always of the physical strength of your characters, for boys and girls are hero worshipers. But more than the physical, magnify the spiritual strength and courage, and hold that up for imitation.

III. THE APPROACH.

The approach to the whole story is the first part of your story, but we have left its consideration until last because that is the order which will usually be followed in actual practice. After you know your story, have determined upon a theme—then, and only then, are you in a position to work out the best approach.

Whether it is the matter of an approach to the story as a whole or to new truth contained in it, the old rule is still the best one: Begin with the known and proceed step by step to the related unknown. The wise teacher will seek to know the mental equipment of each pupil so as to be able to discover and use that "something" to which new and hitherto untaught truth may be likened. Someone has said that the three conditions of good teaching are: first, ASSOCIATION; second, ASSOCIATION; third, ASSOCIATION. It is true. Make your approach on the basis of the known and associate the new and unknown with it.

As you prepare each lesson, search for some potential point of interest in the story which may be linked to some

interest in the pupil's life. INTEREST IS THE BASIS
OF ATTENTION. This makes it necessary for us to link
a point of interest in the lesson to a kindred interest of
the child.

Here is a good example of how a new body of truth is
made clear by an approach through the pupil's interests:
A teacher was teaching the lesson of the plagues and had
hit upon the plan of approaching the lesson by suggesting
that a great game had been played in Egypt. Moses was
the captain of one team, Pharaoh of the other. Each
plague was an inning of the game, and each plague was
studied regarding its effect on Pharaoh, the result being
chalked up against him. After the ninth plague, the
questions were asked, "Who won?" and "Why?" The
teacher questioned, "Can anyone win against God?"
The class was ready with the answer, "No! We must be
on God's team to win." Then came the closing moment
when the teacher asked each one, "Are you on God's
side?"

The next day, one of the boys was asked when it was
that Pharaoh said that Israel might go across the river
to worship. The boy answered, "In the eighth inning."
The teacher had succeeded in approaching the lesson by
linking new truth with a game which was familiar to the
class of boys, and the truth was fixed in their minds. This
particular approach, by its very nature, necessarily affected the whole presentation from approach through application.

An Object as an Initial Approach

As you prepare your story, ask yourself this question:
"What object is there at hand that I may use to arouse
the curiosity of my class as I begin this lesson?" Keep
your eyes open. Your home, the dime stores, the novelty
shops, all are sources of useful curiosity-awakening objects which you may employ as an approach to the lesson.

The value of this type of approach is that it has more
curiosity value than the approach through the ear gate
alone. Curiosity is the means of securing interest. No

curiosity usually means no interest. Curiosity can be deepened into interest, and interest is the key to attention. Without attention there can be no learning. Curiosity is the first step leading upwards to the temple of knowledge. The full stairway is Curiosity, Interest, Attention, Knowledge. You must lead your pupils along this way.

TELLING THE BIBLE STORY
Be Prepared

At the risk of being charged with emphasizing unduly the subject of preparation, we dare to mention it once again: You can tell the story only as well as you have prepared it. Be sure that you have done all that you can possibly do by way of preparation, for more than any other thing, preparation determines your effectiveness. Be so well prepared that you have no need of a quarterly, or lesson leaflet, or notes to guide you. Be so thoroughly prepared that your story is a very part of you and *must* be told.

Have something to say. This is the crux of the whole matter. Have at your command a wealth of interesting material. This is the secret of good story-telling. There is nothing which will give you poise, self-possession, calmness, fluency of speech, as this: to know what you have to say.

Be Imaginative

The teacher's imagination must be constantly in evidence in teaching. Like teacher, like class, in this regard. The imaginative teacher will soon have a class that is imaginative—and that is growing, both in the Word and in numbers. How may you cultivate the imagination in teaching? By using it. Use what you have, and as you use it, study to improve what you have.

Study the art of story-telling. Get a good book of Bible stories and study them as models. Learn one and try telling it. Observe others critically. Never be content with your stage of development. Keep trying to improve.

Study the background of Bible history and geography

and be alert for opportunities to weave in legitimate facts and "local color."

Use the Bible

The Bible itself should be much in evidence as you tell your story. After all, it is a true story and its source is the Word of God. Although you are "giving the sense" in language and terms that your audience of children can grasp, it is still God's message to them. Let the Book have the place of honor.

Even though you propose to tell the story in your own manner, using the vocabulary of children, begin with the reading of a short passage of two or three verses. It helps to establish the source and authority of your story-message. As you have occasion, read from your Bible from time to time. This brings your group back to the Word itself.

Hold your Bible in your hands as much as you can. If you have flannelgraph figures to use in visualizing the story, have a stand, a table, or even a chair, upon which to keep them so that you can hold your Bible in readiness for your frequent reference to it. If you need to lay it down as your hands become otherwise occupied, be sure to take it up at the earliest convenient opportunity. Keep your Bible central in your story by every means and device that you can employ.

Use Visual Aids

Children are attracted by bright colors. Pictures of action capture their interest. Movement and action at the teaching-center keep their eyes on the teacher—and where the eye attends, so does the ear. Therefore, use visual aids as much as possible. The flannelgraph is the ideal in this regard. The scene as it is built up not only attracts, but it involves physical movement on your part, and this draws attention. Objects that may be held before the class are available from many sources—introduce several which may be made to bear on your story. Pictures from magazines, Scripture calendars, and out-of-date Sunday School picture rolls, are valuable visual aids. Collect them and use them. Flash cards, with a simple diagram on one side and a picture on the other, are not difficult to make, and they are good tools.

Try to introduce several of these visual aids in each lesson. It will keep you in motion, and the motion will tend to hold the eye. More than this, each visual aid you use becomes another memory hook by which your lesson-story is secured in your pupil's mind.

Ask Questions

Find out how much your pupils know. Ask questions. Do this to test your teaching at each step. If the pupil cannot give back the teaching in his own words, he has not learned it. Distinguish between your dull and bright pupils and get down to the level of your class. You dare not take anything for granted. You must ask questions which will reveal their knowledge.

Ask questions, too, in order to vary your presentation. Instead of making a positive assertion, phrase it in question form so that a "yes" or "no" answer is called for. A slight nod or shake of your head as you ask it will suggest the correct answer. This brings the class into active participation in the story and is one more gate by which truth enters their minds.

Be Dramatic

Learn to act the parts of the characters. Build the ark! Set up the Tabernacle! Slay Goliath! Use dialogue as much as possible, speaking softly or forcefully as the sense requires. Children love action, so move about with your characters. If space is limited so that you cannot change your position, at least turn with your change from one character to another.

Watch your voice. Monotones are deadly. Loud—soft, fast—slow; change your pace from time to time as the story permits.

Use those hands! They are valuable dramatic tools. With them you may suggest emotions, actions, decisions. Introduce gestures at every turn, but let them be natural, the result of your entering into the part of each character. Do not force them, or they may become unreal.

Be Brief

Let your story be only as long as will hold the attention of your group. Don't try to force your story beyond this point; rather, use the time for something else, an object lesson, perhaps. Twenty or thirty minutes is average for the grade-school child. Beyond that it is difficult for him to give attention. It isn't his fault—it's just a fact of childhood.

Be Dependent

Finally, be dependent. Depend wholly upon the Lord. Methods, as we are giving them to you, are helpful. They will enhance your work. But first, last and always, it is the Lord speaking through you as a channel, who reaches the hearts of boys and girls. Let Him work!

Chapter V.

LET'S PREPARE A STORY

We come now to an exercise designed to show you how to put into actual use the principles and methods you have been studying. Step by step, we shall construct a story, following the pattern of studying and planning we have just considered. The story is that concerning Mephibosheth, son of Jonathan.

The passages of Scripture which have an immediate bearing on the story of Mephibosheth are: I Samuel 20:15; I Samuel 31:1-7; II Samuel 4:4; II Samuel 9; II Samuel 16:1-4; II Samuel 19:24-30; II Samuel 21:7. Let us turn to them and read them, not in the order given, but in the order in which we should probably encounter them in the normal course of study.

NARRATIVE

First of all, let us read for the narrative. What is the story about?

Since the first mention of Mephibosheth is in II Samuel 4:4, let us turn to the passage. In it we learn that Mephibosheth, son of Jonathan and grandson of King Saul, when about five years old, was dropped by his nurse and was crippled for life. The occasion was the coming of tidings out of Jezreel concerning Saul and Jonathan. The nature of the tidings caused the nurse to flee in such haste that the little lad fell, permanently injuring himself.

What was the nature of these tidings? The verse does not tell us, therefore we must read a cross-reference found in the marginal references in our study Bible. (Of course, you will be sure to use a reference Bible in your study.)

We turn, then, to I Samuel 31:1-7. Here is the cause for the alarm. The Philistines had engaged Israel in battle at Mount Gilboa and had put them to rout. In the battle, Saul and his sons, Jonathan included, were killed. When the men of Israel saw that defeat had come upon them, they forsook their cities and fled, the victorious Philistines entering and occupying them. This was the disastrous news, with the terrifying fear of total disaster, that caused Mephibosheth's nurse such concern.

The next reference is II Samuel 9. King David, having succeeded Saul, after his successful wars against the enemies of Israel, turns his thoughts to other obligations. "Is there yet any that is left of the house of Saul, that I may shew him kindness for Jonathan's sake?"

We cannot understand what follows in chapter 9 of II Samuel unless we take up a new trail given in the marginal references. It is I Samuel 20:15, in which David is entreated by Jonathan to enter into a covenant with him to the end that David shall show continued kindness to his house throughout David's lifetime, even though Jonathan may die.

Now back to II Samuel 9.

David's inquiry results in his learning of the existence of Mephibosheth through information supplied by Ziba, formerly servant of Saul. Mephibosheth, says Ziba, is living in the house of Machir, son of Ammiel, in Lodebar. He is lame in both his feet.

David brings Mephibosheth, now grown to manhood, and his son to his house in Jerusalem. He gives all the property of Saul to him and commands Ziba to care for it in his interest. Mephibosheth is given the place of a son in David's household, so that he eats continually at the king's table.

The next bit of history is found in II Samuel 16:1-4. It is the time of Absalom's revolt. David has fled from Jerusalem and is descending on the far side of the Mount of Olives when Ziba, bringing saddled asses and food for the use of the king and his party, overtakes him. When asked about Mephibosheth, Ziba tells David that he has remained behind expecting to be made king over Israel.

David believes this and gives to Ziba all of Mephibosheth's estate.

There is another side to this story, however—Mephibosheth's. The account is found in II Samuel 19:24-30. When, upon David's return to Jerusalem, he is met by Mephibosheth, he learns that what Ziba has told him was utterly untrue.

One more passage—it is II Samuel 21:7. When certain of the family of Saul were delivered over to the Gibeonites for execution, David spared Mephibosheth because of his covenant with Jonathan.

This is the narrative as we have gathered it from the various passages we have studied.

CHARACTERS

Now for the characters. We have already encountered them; but let us examine them more closely. Who are they? What are they like?

David. King David is first, of course. Really, to know David you should take an evening and read I and II Samuel. Read them through as you would the latest book-of-the-month. Even though you are well acquainted with him, it would be good to scan the two Books for the purpose of renewing your acquaintance firsthand.

Mephibosheth. Mephibosheth is our leading character. The things in the story happen to *him.* We will tell the story from his viewpoint.

Mephibosheth seems to be a humble, reverent and properly appreciative person. He is perfectly calm and wholly free from vindictiveness when faced with Ziba's treachery.

Ziba. A character weak in moral fiber and unscrupulous, he seems to be alert for opportunity to advance his own interests. His character must be seen against the background of his libel of his master to David.

The Nurse. All we know about the nurse is found in a single verse where she is mentioned. This is also true of *Micha,* Mephibosheth's son.

Machir, son of Ammiel, was a Gadite sheik living in
Lodebar near Mahanaim. It was in his house that Mephibosheth was sheltered until he was called to Jerusalem.

Incidental Characters, such as Jonathan, Saul, Absalom,
servants, and others, whose lives and deeds contribute to
the understanding of the story, must likewise be considered, but we leave this to you. Actually, no story can be
completely understood without a thorough investigation
of the life and times of every person whose life touches it.

ACTION AND CONFLICT

What are the conflicts? This is our next reading goal.
Several are outstanding. We hardly need to do more than
point them out.

There is the incident out of which Mephibosheth came,
lamed for life. Here is drama—real drama. We shall capitalize on it in the telling of the story, developing the inward conflicts of the nurse, her doubts and fears. The
outward conflicts we shall use, too—her flight in haste
from before the Philistines, her struggle with the injured
lad.

Surely, we will want to take note of the conflict and
action which gave rise to all this—the Philistines' victory
in battle over the armies of Saul.

The next bit of action is the bringing of Mephibosheth
before David. Perhaps there is a conflict here; for when
we consider the subsequent perfidy of Ziba, we are led to
wonder if David's unexpected grant of all of Saul's estate
to Mephibosheth, perhaps at the servant Ziba's expense,
did not give rise to a measure of jealousy. Whether we will
develop this latter hypothetical conflict or not will depend largely upon the theme of our story. And we are
not quite ready for that.

Next in our outline of the action of the narrative is the
revolt of Absalom. We mention it only in passing.

Finally, there is the temporarily successful attempt of
Ziba to supplant Mephibosheth. There is near tragedy
here, and much conflict. But don't become too engrossed

in it; we may not use it, after all. It will all depend upon
how we state our theme.

SCENES

Now, just what are our scenes? Do they not follow the
pattern of the action and conflict? They do. However, do
not forget to use the imagination. Let us take all the
material we have gathered and see how it may be divided
into well-defined scenes that are "fitly framed together."
We might make our scenic division after the following
fashion:

Scene I.   David and Jonathan making their cove-
             nant.

Scene II.   Death of Saul and his sons.

Scene III.   The crippling of Mephibosheth.

Scene IV.   David inquiring after the house of Saul
             and learning of Mephibosheth's existence.

Scene V.   Mephibosheth before David.

Scene VI.   David's flight before Absalom, and Ziba's
             indictment of Mephibosheth.

Scene VII.   Mephibosheth's defense upon the return
             of David.

Scene VIII. David sparing Mephibosheth from ex-
             ecution at the hands of the Gibeonites.

MOVEMENT AND GESTURES

Now it is time to look into each of these scenes in detail so that we may observe what each character is doing.
Suppose we do this with Scene IV for the purpose of
illustration, trusting you to follow through with the same
procedure in those that remain.

II Samuel 9:1-4. David is seated, deep in thought, chin
cradled in his hands. Suddenly he speaks, inquiring if
there is anyone left of the house of Saul. A servant leaves
the room to return later followed by Ziba. Ziba approach-
es David and assumes an attitude of reverence and respect
as they engage in conversation. As Ziba tells David that

Mephibosheth is in Lodebar, he probably points in that general direction.

Study this scene further for yourself and see what more of movement and gesturing you can see in it with imagination's eye. Then go on to the other scenes and study them for movements and gestures.

BACKGROUND

By this time you are sufficiently acquainted with the material that the Bible has presented to you concerning Mephibosheth, and you are in a position to secure real assistance from your lesson "helps." Turn now to whatever you may have in the way of commentaries, dictionaries, or other study aids, using them as checks upon your own study. Take note of any new material they present.

It is beginning to shape up in your mind, isn't it? That is, if you have really been studying the text of the Word of God, not merely reading this guide!

But we aren't ready yet to tell our story—we have only gathered together the materials for it. Suppose we take them now and see what we can do to build them into a Bible-story message.

PLANNING THE STORY OF MEPHIBOSHETH

In surveying the materials we have been gathering for the story of Mephibosheth, we have followed his career through the Scripture passages which tell us about him. The passages we have considered represent the sum total of what is said about him in the Bible. It is supposed that you are familiar with the background of his time, either by previous research or by just now having turned to your helps.

Now the question arises, shall we incorporate all of this material into the story? It can be done. Or, shall we select some and eliminate the rest?

Actually, there is material enough for two stories. Suppose we select only a part of the material—that having to do with Mephibosheth's being brought into the household of the king.

What is this like? Is it not like the introduction into the household of God of the lame, helpless, alienated child of Adam? Why was Mephibosheth so honored? Not for his own sake, but because of David's love for Jonathan and Jonathan's plea for his protection of his family. Isn't this like another grand aspect of our faith—that God for Christ's sake has forgiven us and has reconciled us unto Himself?

If we follow along this line, we see a consistent theme almost ready-made, which the narrative material we have chosen will carry very well. But what of the rest? What of the revolt of Absalom and Ziba's treachery? What of the clearing of Mephibosheth when the true facts are brought out? Surely there is truth that this will portray. There is, but we do not need it, at least for our present purposes. The work isn't lost—it was a necessary part of the process. And it may be that when you have set up your first story, you will desire to develop the unused material into a sequel.

THEME

Now for the statement of the theme. It suggests itself: As David for Jonathan's sake was kind toward Mephibosheth, so God for Christ's sake bestows His grace on us.

SCENES

Now for division of the material we have chosen into scenes. What is left after our elimination of the material which we cannot use for our present purposes? As previously set forth, it consists of five scenes.

Scene I. David and Jonathan making their covenant.

Scene II. The death of Saul and his sons.

Scene III. The crippling of Mephibosheth.

Scene IV.   David's inquiry after the house of Saul
and his learning of Mephibosheth's existence.

Scene V.   Mephibosheth before David.

Do we want to leave them in this order? Can we arrange
them to better advantage? Conceivably, we might take any
one of the first four scenes as a springboard into the action
of the story. Which will give us the most interesting opening?

Why not begin with Scene III? It has potentialities for
interest that none of the others has—suspense, anxiety,
danger, disaster. The single verse, of necessity, must be
amplified by legitimate inventions, but the framework is
there.

Then, too, we can combine Scene II with it by an explanatory "flash-back," or by putting the whole into the
mouth of a servant who bursts on the scene with the news
of the Philistines' successful invasion.

The same sort of combination can be effected by incorporating Scene I into Scene IV, perhaps by a similar
device.

Scene V must stand alone.

We have now just three major scenes for our story, although by bringing in the explanatory material in sub-
scenes, all five have been incorporated into the story. How
does it look now? Here is the way the scenes will shape
up as we tell the story, weaving in background material
and legitimate inventions:

Scene I

Jonathan's home. Five-year-old Mephibosheth and his
nurse are playing a game when a breathless servant bursts
in on them with the dreadful news out of Jezreel that the
conquering Philistines are on the march, overrunning the
cities of Israel. Saul is dead! Mephibosheth's father is
dead! They must run for their lives.

The nurse, in her haste to depart, stumbles with Mephibosheth. The force of the fall disables him so that the

nurse must carry him as they flee. They make their way quickly to the house of Machir, son of Ammiel, in Lodebar, where Mephibosheth finds refuge.

Scene II

King David is seated in his house at Jerusalem. Since the death of Saul, he has been occupied with the great task of consolidating his kingdom. He has subdued the enemies of Israel, and the Lord has given him rest.

In this time of peace, David's thoughts turn to earlier days. He thinks of his covenant with Jonathan in Ramah. He had promised Jonathan that he would always show kindness to his family. But he had been so much at war that he had not done it. Now the years have slipped away. Is there any one left of the house of Saul? If there is, he will fulfill his promise.

Ziba, a former servant of Saul, is brought before him. Yes, Ziba says, there is a son of Jonathan who is lame. He lives in Lodebar with Machir, son of Ammiel.

The orders are given. Mephibosheth is to be brought to Jerusalem so that David may show him kindness for Jonathan's sake.

Scene III

Mephibosheth, ushered into David's presence, falls on his face in reverence before the king. David speaks to him. He tells him of his covenant with his father, Jonathan. Now he will do what he had promised. All of Saul's land is to be given to him. Ziba, formerly servant of Saul, with his fifteen sons and twenty servants, shall till the land for him.

But more than all this, David tells the lame Mephibosheth, he is to take his place at the king's table as one of the king's sons. So Mephibosheth—helpless, alienated Mephibosheth—through no merit of his own, but solely because of David's covenant with Jonathan, dwells in Jerusalem, eating at the king's table.

THE APPLICATIONS

By this time you have settled on the major application which very naturally follows the theme we have chosen. And, no doubt, you have taken note of many opportunities to drive home gospel applications as you have followed the development of the three scenes of our story. What are they? Let us list them.

The Major Application. Remember the theme we chose: As David for Jonathan's sake was gracious toward Mephibosheth, so God for Christ's sake bestows His grace on us. With such a theme we can have no other major application than this, that God longs to take us into His family, make us His sons, and all because of our Lord Jesus Christ. We could hardly do better in stating our major application than to take the theme itself!

Minor Applications. Let us not "go everywhere, preaching the gospel" as we tell this story, lest we destroy, or at least impair, its unity. Not all possible applications, but those which support the major one, are what we mainly seek.

Go back and review the final form our scenes took. What likenesses to gospel truth do you see?

Scene I. The crippling of Mephibosheth suggests our own inability to walk with God. At the close of the scene we will stress the helplessness of the unsaved person. Then, there is the alienation of Mephibosheth. He spends his years away from the courts of the king. Our natural alienation from God immediately comes to mind. Suppose we settle on these two for Scene I.

Scene II. As we consider Jonathan's plea to David, there comes to mind the prayer of our Lord in John 17, especially verse 20: "Neither pray I for these alone, but for them also which shall believe on me through their word," as seen in the light of the whole chapter.

Then, there is the call for Mephibosheth to come to Jerusalem. What if he had chosen not to heed it? Here is an application we can use at the very close of our story in our final plea.

Scene III. Since this scene is the climax of the whole story, the major application will be made at its close. There is, however, a minor one suggested by the words of Mephibosheth in II Samuel 9:8: "What is thy servant, that thou shouldest look upon such a dead dog as I am?" Ephesians 2:1 sums up the application we might make here. We shall plan to use it.

THE APPROACH

What shall be the approach? Since the whole story is the approach to the truth it will embody, we need spend but little time here. Why not, then, try an object?

A cane, a crutch, the picture of a wheel chair—any of these would serve to secure attention during our opening words. Or, to follow another train of associations, two pictures—one of a nomad's tent, the other of a palace—would serve to hold the eye as you introduce the story of the lame boy who was brought from a similar tent in Lodebar to a new home in the palace of a king. (Look through back numbers of the *National Geographic Magazine* for suitable pictures.)

We are ready now for the weaving of our story. We have settled upon the matter and we have abundant material at our disposal. Here is one way the story might be told:

THE STORY OF MEPHIBOSHETH

Would you like it if you were to be injured so that you couldn't run or play? Would you like to be taken out of a nice home, away from your family, to grow up among strangers, lame and helpless? This happened to a boy named Mephibosheth. Listen to his story:

It was long, long ago in the days of Israel's first king, Saul, that Mephibosheth, son of Jonathan, was born. King Saul was his grandfather. Mephibosheth, you see, was the son of a prince, and the grandson of a king!

Because his father, Jonathan, was the son of King Saul, Mephibosheth lived in a fine home and had everything his heart could desire. He had a nurse who did nothing else but care for him and play with him. During the time when his father was away with his army fighting the fierce Philistines, she played with him more than ever.

One day word came that the Philistines were invading the land. Jonathan and his men of war were needed in Gilboa. Don't you suppose that Jonathan went into the room where little five-year-old Mephibosheth was playing with his nurse to see him before he left for the battle?

"Take good care of him, Nurse," Jonathan must have said. "He is dearer than life to me. Care for him and protect him at all costs. And if the Philistines should come, flee for your lives!"

Soon after Jonathan left, word came back that the godless Philistines were camped in Shunem—Israel's army was gathered at Gilboa. How eagerly Mephibosheth and his nurse must have awaited each messenger as he came with a fresh bit of news for them! Now the Philistines are at Aphek, the Israelites at Jezreel! And then—the armies clashed! The battle is on!

The most terrible news comes to Mephibosheth's home. Perhaps a special messenger comes running and breathlessly gasps out his message.

"The Philistines are coming; run for your lives! They are entering the cities. Hurry! Hurry! You have little time. They are on the way here."

"What of Jonathan? Give us news of Jonathan."

"Dead—Jonathan is slain. Saul is slain. All is lost. The men of Israel are forsaking the cities. The Philistines are taking them all. Take the lad to a place of safety—quickly, you have no time to waste. Away! Away!"

But where is there a place of safety for the grandson of the king? Across Jordan, in the land of Gad? Yes, Mephibosheth will surely find safe refuge there from the slaughtering Philistines.

Swinging Mephibosheth up from the floor into her arms, the nurse turns to flee. Mephibosheth is heavy in her arms. In her haste she stumbles and falls, Mephibosheth striking the pavement with such force that he is unable to get to his feet.

There is no time to stop. Even though Mephibosheth's pain is terrible, they must go on. Gad is far away and the Philistines are swiftly sweeping the land. The long journey down to Jordan must be made and a refuge found for Mephibosheth beyond the river.

They made the journey, despite the many difficulties, despite the injury to Mephibosheth. At last, they are safely across the river Jordan. Now for a home for Mephibosheth.

In the house of Machir, son of Ammiel, at Lodebar the refuge was found. Here Mephibosheth grew up—away from the courts of the king. But the trip had been made at a terrible cost. Although the nurse and Machir did all they could for Mephibosheth, there was no help for him. He would be lame for the rest of his life. He grew up unable to play the outdoor games other boys enjoyed.

How like us, before we are saved! We, too, are helpless—lame; not in our two feet, of course, but spiritually. We cannot walk with God. We cannot walk in His paths. We cannot do the things He would have us do. We are unable to do these things, for sin has crippled us and we are spiritually lame.

How like Mephibosheth we are in this, too—before we believe on the Lord Jesus we are away from God, far away. Just as Mephibosheth was separated from the courts of the king, so we are separated from the things of God and heaven, because of sin.

It is good to know that the moment we believe on the Lord Jesus as our Saviour, that moment God heals our lameness of spirit and says to us, "But now in Christ Jesus ye who sometimes were far off are made nigh by the blood of Christ" (Eph. 2:13).

For many years lame Mephibosheth lived with Machir. He grew to be a man. He married and had a son. And all the while he was growing up, King David was waging war

against the enemies of Israel, subduing them and strengthening the kingdom.

One day King David sat deep in thought in his palace in
Jerusalem. He was thinking about the goodness of God
toward him. "The Lord had given him rest round about
from all his enemies" (II Sam. 7:1). He had given him a
wonderful house. He had made him strong.

David's thoughts, no doubt, turned to the days when he
had been hunted by Saul throughout the land. He had
lived in caves, in the forest, in the fields. Saul had sought
to kill him through jealousy and David had been a fugitive
for years, but now God had given him the throne of the
very one who had long sought his life.

David thought of Jonathan—how they had loved each
other! How Jonathan had given him warning at the stone
Ezel that Saul was still seeking to kill him. Jonathan had
said, "If it please my father to do thee evil, then I will
shew it thee, and send thee away, that thou mayest go in
peace: and the Lord be with thee, as he hath been with
my father. And thou shalt not only while yet I live shew
me the kindness of the Lord, that I die not: but also thou
shalt not cut off thy kindness from my house for ever."

David had promised, for he and Jonathan loved each
other as they loved their own souls. And now many years
had passed, and David had done nothing at all to keep his
covenant. He must keep his word! He had given his promise to Jonathan.

"Servants!" he called. They came running.

"Is there yet any that is left of the house of Saul, that I
may shew him kindness for Jonathan's sake?"

Quickly the word spread. David is seeking any that is
left of the house of Saul. He would show him kindness for
Jonathan's sake!

There is found in Israel a man, Ziba by name, who had
been servant to Saul. He was brought to King David.

"Art thou Ziba?" asked David.

"Thy servant is he," replied Ziba.

"Is there not yet any of the house of Saul, that I may shew the kindness of God unto him?" inquired the king.

Ziba answered, "Jonathan hath yet a son, which is lame on his feet."

"Where is he?"

"In the house of Machir, the son of Ammiel, from Lodebar. His name is Mephibosheth."

"See that he is brought to me," ordered King David. "For Jonathan's sake, who made me promise to shew kindness to his house forever, I will shew Mephibosheth the very kindness of God. Fetch him here at once."

Do you know, boys and girls, David's promise to Jonathan is like another great gospel truth. David had heard Jonathan's plea and, because he loved him as he loved his own soul, had granted it. One day the Lord Jesus Christ prayed in a similar way to God for those who should believe on Him.

He prayed, "And the glory which thou gavest me I have given them; that they may be one, even as we are one: I in them, and thou in me, that they may be made perfect in one; and that the world may know that thou hast sent me, and hast loved them, as thou hast loved me.

"Father, I will that they also, whom thou hast given me, be with me where I am; that they may behold my glory, which thou hast given me: for thou lovedst me before the foundation of the world" (John 17:22-24).

God heard His prayer and is waiting to answer it for you—if you will take the Lord Jesus as your Saviour.

Was there anything in Mephibosheth that would cause David to show kindness to him? No, it was because of David's love for Jonathan. Just so, there is no good in us that would lead God to hear and answer the prayer of our Lord Jesus Christ; but because God loved Him from before the foundation of the world, He is quick to shower His goodness and grace upon us from the moment that we believe on His Son as our Saviour and Sin-Bearer.

Up in the land of Gad at Lodebar the word came to Mephibosheth: "King David is calling you to come to

Jerusalem. He would shew you kindness because of his love for Jonathan, your father."

"But I am lame," Mephibosheth might have said. "I cannot serve in his army. I can be of no use to him. I am helpless."

"No matter!" the reply would be. "David loved your father and he will show you the very kindness of God, for Jonathan's sake. It is his love for Jonathan, not what you can or cannot do for David, that makes him send for you. Will you come? At once?"

Do you suppose that Mephibosheth needed to take much time to decide? No, he surely went at once, taking his son Micha with him. Mephibosheth remembered the first journey he had made. How his poor injured feet had caused him such an agony of pain. He had been fleeing for his life then. Now he is returning to receive the blessing and favor of the king.

At last the party reached Jerusalem. Mephibosheth was announced to the king and ushered into his presence. Immediately, Mephibosheth fell on his face before the king to show his reverence for Israel's ruler.

"Mephibosheth," said David.

"Behold thy servant!" Mephibosheth answered.

"Fear not, Mephibosheth, I will surely shew thee kindness for Jonathan thy father's sake. I loved him, and years ago I promised him that always and forever I would be kind to his house. Stand up, Mephibosheth!"

Mephibosheth slowly and awkwardly rose to his feet.

David spoke again, "For Jonathan's sake I will return to thee all the land of Saul and you shall eat bread at my table continually."

Mephibosheth bowed before David. He didn't deserve all this. David had never known him, had not seen him before. He did not need to do anything for him, lame as he was. He could not enter the service of David—he himself needed to be served. But David had loved Jonathan and had granted Jonathan's plea.

Mephibosheth found it difficult to speak. His voice must have choked as he said, "What is thy servant, that thou shouldest look upon such a dead dog as I am?"

Boys and girls, every one of us is as dead toward God, while we are unsaved, as Mephibosheth counted himself to be toward David. We are "dead in trespasses and sins" (Eph. 2:1), unless we believe on the Lord Jesus Christ, that He may make us alive. Isn't it a wonderful thing that He should want to do even more for us than David did for Mephibosheth?

The king called for Ziba, Saul's servant, to come.

"Ziba," he said, "I have given unto thy master's son all that pertained to Saul and to all his house. Thou therefore, and thy sons (Ziba had fifteen sons), and thy servants (there were twenty of them), shall till the land for him, and thou shalt bring in the fruits, that thy master's son may have food to eat: but Mephibosheth, thy master's son, shall eat bread alway at my table."

Ziba bowed low and spoke in obedience, "According to all that my lord the king hath commanded his servant, so shall thy servant do."

David spoke again: "As for Mephibosheth, he shall eat at my table, as one of the king's sons."

So Mephibosheth lived in Jerusalem and though he was lame and though he had been away in Lodebar for years and years, yet he took his place at the king's table as one of the king's sons.

Boys and girls, just as David, for Jonathan's sake, was gracious toward Mephibosheth, so God, for Christ's sake, bestows His grace on us.

Without the Lord Jesus Christ we are dead in trespasses and sins. We cannot walk with God—we can only walk as Satan would have us walk (Eph. 2:1-2). We are away from God and heaven—just as Mephibosheth was away from the courts of the king.

But God saves us by His grace. "For by grace are ye saved through faith" (Eph. 2:8). He forgives us of every sin "for Christ's sake" (Eph. 4:32); and we, who like

Mephibosheth "were far off are made nigh by the blood of Christ" (Eph. 2:12-13).

You see, boys and girls, the Lord Jesus was God's well-beloved, only-begotten Son. He loved us so much that He was willing to be our substitute so He took the wages of our sin, death. On the cross, God laid on Him all of our sins, so that Jesus bore them in His own body for us. He died for us. God loved the Lord Jesus so much, and was so satisfied with His death for our sin on the cross, that He raised Him from the dead. Now, because God loves the Son, He is willing to save us if we will but receive His Son as a gift.

And, like Mephibosheth who was given the place of a son, we are made sons of God when we take the Lord Jesus as our Saviour. John 1:12: "But as many as received him, to them gave he power to become the sons of God, even to them that believe on his name."

Would Mephibosheth have had the place of a king's son at the king's table if he had refused to obey the call? No, he would have missed it all. Just so, boys and girls, we miss it all if we refuse the call of God to come to the Lord Jesus Christ and receive Him as the One who died for us and rose again. God longs to make us His sons, for Christ's sake, and to bless us with every spiritual blessing in the heavenlies in Him (Eph. 1:3), but He can only do His part as we do our part. And our part is to believe on the name of the Lord Jesus Christ, to receive Him as our Saviour.

Will you, right now, receive Him? Bow your head and ask Him to come into your heart to live there as your very own Saviour.

Chapter VI.

ATTENTION, PLEASE!

"Johnny doesn't pay attention during the lesson," you say of a particularly inattentive boy in your class. Yes, he does. But not to you!

Inattention does not necessarily mean a total lack of attention, but rather that the attention is focused on something other than that to which you desire it to be given. Your task as a teacher is to secure the attention of your class, to hold it even when it tends to wander, and to use it as the powerful teaching essential that it is.

Attention is the mind's great magnifying glass. Like the lens which the boy uses to gather up the rays of the sun and centralize them in one hot, burning spot, attention gathers up the devious rays of thought and focuses them upon a single object.

There are two kinds of attention, voluntary and involuntary. The first is hard work, usually; the second is without effort.

You are sitting in the living room of your home, studying this chapter. A car goes by outside with a great deal of noise. You notice it and, with an effort, turn your thoughts back to the printed page. You notice that the room is overly warm. Another effort of the will brings your attention back. And so it goes—you give attention, by forcing yourself to dismiss this distraction and that, in order to concentrate on your study. This is voluntary attention.

A boy is lying on his stomach on the floor of the same room, reading another book. He is lost in the story. With Huck Finn he is on the Mississippi. He hears no noise, save the lapping of the river's waves on Huck Finn's raft.

He feels no discomfort. You call his name several times before you break through the barrier of his concentration. His attention to the tale he reads is without effort, it is involuntary. He can't help but give attention!

It is involuntary attention, the kind that boys and girls can't help giving, that we want. Frequently it is not until late childhood and early adolescence that the mind can give voluntary attention for any more than a brief period. Even when the mind can compel itself to give attention, it is still true that the mind does its best work when attention is involuntary.

It is quite useless to demand attention—you must secure it and hold it. It is up to you.

Without attention there can be no learning. Unless we are attentive, things "go in one ear and out the other." We can be conscious of many things, but when attention fastens on one of them, it fills the whole scene to the exclusion of all the rest. You are sitting in your favorite chair, reading or relaxing. You are conscious of many things—the radio, the street noises, a jumble of sounds— but you are not really listening to any one of them. Your attention is not being given to any one of them. Suddenly, for apparently no reason, you are concentrating on what the radio is bringing to you. You are paying attention to the speaker. What did he say during the preceding moments? You don't know. You heard him, didn't you? Yes, but your attention was elsewhere, or nowhere. But now you are storing away the information he is passing on to you. You are attentive—you are learning.

Do you see, now, how so much so-called teaching is merely so much talking? The pupil hears you—but he does not attend to what you are saying. It is not teaching unless the pupil gives attention to the truths you teach. He must not only be conscious of them, he must focus attention on them and think them. Until he stocks the truths in his mental storehouse, there is no learning. And if the pupil is not learning, you are not teaching!

I. ATTENTION-DRAWING APPEALS.

It is at once apparent that the teacher, in order to teach and not merely to talk, must fight a constant battle with the many distractions which contest the vantage point of the pupil's attention. It will help us understand better the attention-winning methods which follow, if we first consider the possible appeals which draw attention.

The appeal to the ear. What a whole host of sounds clamor for the attention of the child you would teach. Your competition is fierce. The warfare is constant.

You appeal to the ear whenever you teach. As you present your lesson, the sound of your voice with its various modulations appeals through the ear gate and, to the extent that your appeal is successful, draws attention your way. You ask a question—the appeal is through the ear. Attention fastens upon the question, the mind begins to function, thought processes are stirred into action—and the pupil learns.

The story is the great means of drawing attention toward the truth you would teach. Say: "I heard about a man who—" and pause a moment. You will see your class snap to attention.

The appeal to the eye. More and more are teachers appreciating the value of the eye gate. Memory holds far more of what we see and hear than of what we hear only. The chief value of visual aids, such as the flannelgraph, objects, blackboard diagrams, etc., is that they draw attention to a focus upon the truth being taught.

The cye is much more easily distracted than the ear. Hold the eye and you hold the ear as well. Notice how the curtaining off of Sunday School space—while it doesn't reduce the volume of sound—by shutting out distracting sights accomplishes much the same end. The pupil cannot see the source, so he doesn't have his attention drawn away by the sound.

Experienced teachers use this appeal when, to gain wandering attention, they walk rapidly across the platform, or make a quick gesture, or otherwise suddenly introduce a new motion. Try it sometime.

The appeal to the touch. Herein lies the value of correlated handwork. It demands attention. Whether the handwork is the elaborate reproduction or illustration of truth in some concrete form, or simple notes in an inexpensive notebook, the appeal is the same, through the touch gate.

When all three of these gates are used at the same time, it can be seen that the appeal for attention should be powerful! Perhaps it will not be possible for us to use every possible appeal, but let us always endeavor to use as many as possible on every occasion.

II. ATTENTION-WINNING METHODS.

There are some methods, widely practiced it is true, yet without success, which you will do well to avoid. Threatening will not win attention to your teaching. Scolding will not do it. Even demanding the attention of a pupil or of a class will not help the situation. These methods attract attention to themselves and away from the lesson.

Is it the pupil's fault that he does not pay attention? Whose fault is it? Henry Ward Beecher was asked by the sexton of his church if he should awaken any members of the congregation who might fall asleep during the sermon. "No," the great preacher replied, "come to the pulpit and wake me up." Why not assume the blame for inattention yourself?

Here are some attention-winning methods. Perhaps you have not been using some of them. Study your own methods in their light, with a view to strengthening your whole teaching approach at this first strategic battle—the battle for the pupil's attention.

Try to have the best possible physical conditions. Perhaps an air-conditioned, soundproof room, indirect lighting, furnished with the best of seating and equipment, not too large for your class, not too small, is out of the question. But you can make the best of what you have. Not the "best" but the "best possible" conditions, we said.

Usually you can exercise a measure of control over such conditions as light, heat, ventilation. Do what you can to have these things just right. Shut out hindrances and distractions as far as possible. If you cannot shut out the sound, at least screen off disturbing sights. If you can't have a screen, then turn the seats around so that your class faces away from everything that would tend to draw their attention away from you. Protect the class against interruptions, loud talking, and unnecessarily loud noises.

Be sure that every member of your group can see you clearly and hear you distinctly.

Talk to your class in a conversational manner. While you should avoid speaking directly to a single individual, at the same time you should strive for the intimacy that makes what you say personal to each one. It is embarrassing for one child to be singled out and addressed individually, and the class rather resents the neglect that necessarily results. Your lesson is for the whole class, therefore talk to the class as a whole.

Cultivate the conversational manner. Automatically, the condescending "holy tone," which sometimes creeps into the teacher's style and which is a loathsome plague, will be eliminated. The conversational style makes for attention—the lecturer's approach doesn't, at least among children.

Speak as softly as circumstances will permit. "Like produces like." Suppose yours is a particularly disorderly class. Do you shout to be heard above their noise? Doesn't do much good, does it? Instead of whispering to each other, they talk in undertones—they have to, to be heard above your shouting. Very well, if it doesn't help to shout, then put more effort into it—really shout! Now they must talk, not in undertones, but aloud. Vicious cycle, isn't it?

Use well-modulated tones from the very beginning. It helps to establish the proper atmosphere for listening attentively. Most boys and girls will react favorably and will respond accordingly.

But suppose the effect doesn't last and attention begins to wander? Still you haven't exhausted all the possibilities of a soft voice. Drop down to a whisper and stay there until that youngster in the back row notices the unusual and removes his attention from whatever it is that he is doing and gives it back to you. It will work— try it and see.

Let the pupils participate. Wouldn't you yourself find it dull if you were seated in a discussion group but were not permitted to speak when you disagreed? Suppose you were not privileged to ask a question when a point is not clear. How would you react? Wouldn't it be easy for your mind to wander so that your attention would be fastened on other things?

The teacher should encourage the members of the class to raise questions and otherwise to enter into the discussion. If your class is backward in this regard, ask the questions yourself and encourage the class to answer them.

Do you need an illustration for some point? Ask the class to supply it. Of course, you will have one ready to use if the class fails to provide one, and you will make it seem to be their contribution by drawing it out of them by means of leading questions.

Set up theoretical situations which call for decisions, then ask them to decide what they would do if faced with such a problem.

When the youngster's mind is kept busy in this way, it can hardly become attentive to other things that are irrelevant to the matter at hand.

Use visual aids. This doesn't mean that you should possess and use elaborate equipment for the projection of slides or movies. It doesn't mean that you should own the finest felt scenic backgrounds and figures for the flannelgraph. It doesn't mean that you must concentrate on elaborate object lessons. But it does mean that you must use the eye gate, somehow.

Visual aids may be quite simple and still be effective. An air mail envelope from Brazil, a hammer, a candle, a nest of colored blocks, a few pieces of colored yarn or ribbon, a coin, a piece of currency—things like these, when linked to the truth taught, may be quite effective aids.

The flannelgraph is excellent as an aid. Workers should capitalize on its eye gate appeal. There is hardly a lesson that cannot be given visual aid by use of this device.

The test of the value of any object or device as a visual aid is whether or not it can gather and hold the attention of the pupil so that the lesson is learned—and so taught!

Change your program. Don't do the same things in the same way week after week. Change your method of teaching, or your type of visual aid, frequently. Don't get in a rut and stay there. Change the way you handle incidental details, such as, the attendance record, the offering, or the missionary emphasis.

Children appreciate change. Watch them as they take a new "short cut" to school. Never mind that it is really a longer route, it provides a thrilling change. Notice how they love to exchange clothing for the sake of wearing something different.

Change your routine frequently and you will avoid monotony, the source of much inattention.

If your group is of the primary or beginner age, change is especially important. Every few minutes have them change activities, exchange seats, or otherwise vary the course of things for them. Activity of body is an essential at their particular stage of development. You must supply such opportunity for movement of their little, growing, restless bodies by such changes.

There is a limit; stay within it. There is a definite limit to the time a youngster can give sustained attention to any single thing without relief. The younger the child the briefer the span of his attention. It is foolish to expect to hold attention for a longer time than the child can give it, if you do not introduce relief that is needed.

The average primary group is able to give attention to any single thing for approximately twenty minutes. In the junior age group the span is longer—about thirty minutes. If you exceed these limits, attention is either divided or it lacks depth and intensiveness.

If you can discover the attention span of your class and adapt your program accordingly, you will do much to prevent inattention. Suppose, however, that yours is a Sunday School class whose attention span is eighteen minutes. You have a class period of thirty minutes. You are not in a position to have a "program" but are limited to the teaching of the lesson—that, and that alone. How can you accommodate yourself to such a situation?

Try this: Do your actual teaching at the very first, the first eighteen minutes. Then, when attention tends to wander, stimulate it with questions, illustrations, and applications supplied by the class itself. This will provide something different enough to permit the class to launch out on another attention span.

Praise your class when they are attentive. There is no stronger stimulant to improvement in any respect than praise for progress made. When your class has been attentive, even though it has endured but a little while, praise them for it. Tell them how good it is to teach such an attentive group. This is better, much better, than scolding.

Prepare thoroughly. Have your program so thoroughly prepared that you have no need of notes. When you must refer frequently to notes, or when you r ust take time to search for a passage whose location isn't certain, the class's continuity of thought is broken and inattention sets in.

Thorough preparation, as careful and complete as you can make it, will do much to keep things moving so that attention won't have opportunity to wander away.

Be dramatic. Do not be afraid to use gestures. Do not be afraid to act out your lesson story. Put yourself into the part of every character who comes on the scene. Movement draws attention.

Be Peter warming himself at the fire in the courtyard. When you tell how the Lord knocks for admission at our hearts' doors, actually knock on your breast. Characters become living persons when you so portray them, and it is much easier for the class to give attention to some such interesting presentation than to a dull recitation of facts, however worth-while they may be.

Reduce interruptions to a minimum. When a train of thought is broken, it is more difficult to re-establish attention than it was to capture it at the beginning. Don't let attention to class records, for instance, provide opportunity for interruption. So organize the incidentals—the "necessary evils"—that full attention may be given to the chief item—the lesson.

Don't see too much! It is better to ignore the minor inattention of one person than to distract the attention of the entire class by rebuking him. Only if the child is annoying another, should you recognize the situation and take corrective measures. But if the youngster is not disturbing, it is the course of wisdom to ignore his inattention. Why disturb the rest, whose attention you have?

Sometimes when a pupil is corrected for some tangible evidence of inattention, the rest of the class takes up the same thing! A teacher rebukes one boy for swinging his legs a bit too vigorously, whereupon all legs begin to swing! Before suggesting leg-swinging by calling attention to it, the rest of the class had been intently listening to her lesson.

So, don't see too much. You can afford to overlook many of the lesser inattentions.

One word more before leaving the subject of methods that win attention. It is this: If one thing fails to produce the desired attention in an inattentive group, drop it and try something new.

III. ATTENTION-HOLDING ATTRACTIONS.

Turn now to the consideration of principles. There are some fundamental principles that govern the holding of attention. There are certain attractions that hold attention as the magnet holds the bit of steel. What are they?

The Attraction of Curiosity. Hold up a curio before your class and hear the inevitable question, "What is that?" Attention follows curiosity as surely as morning follows sunrise. But the burden of deepening casual curiosity into sustained attention is upon the teacher.

You may awaken curiosity by an appeal to the eye, by a question, or simply by the expression, "Once upon a time . . ." Curiosity is immediately aroused and attention is turned your way.

A well-directed question will always awaken curiosity. Ask your class, "What is the fifteenth book in the Old Testament?" and watch them begin to count!

But beware of satisfying curiosity too fully or too soon. It must be deepened into interest if the attention it brings is to continue.

Never, under any circumstances, suppress this mental hunger—for that is what curiosity is. Stimulate it, use it, satisfy it, for unless there is this "appetite of the mind" to receive truth, it is useless to attempt to teach.

The Attraction of Interest. People give attention to the things they are interested in. Interest is the great key to attention. It is because of this that we proceed from the known to the unknown. We put the old in a new setting, or the new in an old setting for the same reason. In preparing a lesson, search for some point of interest which may be linked to a kindred interest in the pupil's experience.

While we will probably never achieve such teaching perfection as to no longer need to appeal to the individual to give voluntary attention, yet, by using the attraction of interest, voluntary attention may become involuntary and real learning will follow with such ease and effortlessness that we marvel!

Remember that interest is the mother of attention. Attention is the mother of knowledge. To secure knowledge you must secure both attention and interest.

The Attraction of the Unusual. We remember the strange things we have seen, the strange places we have visited, the strange sounds we have heard. It is not difficult to give attention to the unusual.

Therefore, present your lesson's truths in an unusual way. We never forget the stories of soldiers and heroes—about battles, wounds and death. Nor do we forget the stories of missionaries. How difficult it is to lose the lesson that is illustrated by an unusual yet appropriate story!

Be alert for illustrations which will appeal to every sense in the giving of them—sight, hearing, touch, taste, smell. Use words in the telling which will arouse these senses.

For the purpose of illustration, we now speak to you about sucking a great big, juicy, yellow lemon. There is a queer sensation at the root of your tongue, isn't there? Isn't it because there has been an arousing of taste sense by a simple suggestion? It is this sort of thing, in every avenue of the sense, that you should look for in illustrations. It will make them unusual; and the unusual attracts.

The Attraction of Variety. Avoid sameness as you would the plague. We might as well face the fact squarely that attention cannot be sustained indefinitely. Attention is easily satisfied and flits to something else unless something new is constantly developing.

You must introduce variety into your teaching. Appeal to the eye by using visual aids. Appeal to the ear by using stories and questions. Appeal to the sense of touch through appropriate handwork.

It is as easy to fall into a monotony of routine as it is a monotony of speech. Avoid both. Variety, contrast, change of pace—these are the things for which you should constantly strive if you would hold attention.

The Attraction of the Familiar. It is true that there is little attraction in that which is so familiar as to be commonplace. Yet there is attraction in the familiar.

Have you ever traveled a new route through a familiar countryside? You are interested, of course. You are giving a measure of your divided attention to the countryside. It is no different, however, from many similar scenes you have seen in the vicinity. Suddenly, your attention is arrested! That house and barn—they look familiar. Why, you recognize them; you remember them, although you had never before seen them from the present viewpoint. Now you are all attention, looking for other recognizable objects. The attraction of the familiar has taken hold of your attention.

Don't hesitate to use familiar material. Stories do not suffer by repetition at not too frequent intervals, but rather are more effective than when first given. The youngster is alert for action he knows to be just ahead. He will give attention to the familiar. Children love to sing the familiar songs (don't we all?) and hymns. They have their favorites of which they seem never to tire.

In the search for variety and the unusual, for the things which will arouse curiosity—do not discount the value of the familiar.

The Attraction of Association. Since only what the pupil attends to will be really learned, you must use language and illustrations in line with their interests. Adaptation to their level of experience and association with their interests are the rules.

A soldier was asked to take a class of boys one Sunday. He not only "took" the class but he taught the class. The superintendent noticed that the usually noisy class was unusually silent. Looking in, he saw the veteran telling the boys how he had suffered for his country. Then he told the boys how Christ had been wounded for them. This was adaptation and association. Do you suppose the class ever forgot?

Finally, there is the Attraction of Participation. Boys and girls love to do things. Let them have an active part in the presentation of the lesson. It may be that they will respond to well-directed questions. Frequent dramatizations of a simple kind are excellent. The writer once brought an entire department into active participation on the teaching of the Tabernacle by having the group go outdoors, measure actual distances, and then form a living outline of the Tabernacle and its chief features. He will never forget the lessons that were learned that day, and he doubts that any who participated will ever forget.

Pass those objects around. Let the youngsters put the figures on the flannelboard for you. Let them ask, and answer, questions. By whatever means or device, let them participate.

Chapter VII.

YOUR DISCIPLINE PROBLEM

They will manage you if they can! And they are ingenious when it comes to taking advantage of every opportunity to take charge of a gathering at your expense. Where boys and girls gather together, there is a potential discipline problem.

Your problem may be only an occasional one; or it may be chronic. Perhaps it may involve a single individual; perhaps the entire class is guilty. Then, it may be a matter of willful and malicious misbehavior; or it could be nothing more serious than sprightly mischief. But it is a problem—and it can hinder the teaching of the class.

Suppose we follow a plan of attack designed to alleviate, if not to eliminate completely, this problem. The plan is simply this: Find the culprit; discover the causes; apply the necessary correctives; arrange a crisis; observe certain cautions all the while.

FIND THE CULPRIT

There really are not many culprits to track down; there are but three. They are circumstances, the child, and yourself. Someone or something is to blame if you have a discipline problem. Before we can do much else, we must track down the guilty one and bring him to the light, that we might go beyond him to the underlying causes of his delinquency.

It may be circumstances.

Perhaps your quarters are inadequate, or conducive to inattention—that archenemy which is father to so much difficulty, especially discipline problems.

Overcrowding, for instance, has a direct bearing on mis-behavior. It is nearly impossible to maintain perfect order if you have twenty youngsters uncomfortably quartered where only fifteen could be cared for without crowding.

Poorly shielded quarters which fail to shut off the sight and sound of other activities may be to blame. The children are distracted from your program, largely because of their inability to give sustained voluntary attention when so much else clamors for their ears and lures their eyes.

Don't be in a hurry, however, to ask for a new building. You see, it could be the weather. For weather, too, is a factor to be considered. There are problem "seasons" when difficulty mounts.

Neither should you hasten to attach all the blame to circumstances. This culprit isn't the only one who might be to blame. As a matter of fact, it isn't the usual one.

It may be the children.

Are they to blame? We are inclined to blame them first, aren't we? And, I suppose, justly so. After all, they should not be unruly. To the extent that they present a discipline problem, either as individuals or as a class, they are to blame.

But let's be sure. It is possible that the other culprits really should be indicted. Don't dispose of the problem by being less than sympathetically understanding of the child's susceptibility to misbehavior when there is break-down in other directions. It's pretty much his nature at certain times and at certain stages of development to be a problem child if the incentive and opportunity are pro-vided at one and the same time.

Don't decide the issue for a while. There is another suspect to be brought to trial, and we have yet really to re-view the entire case of every suspect. This is what the police would call a "morning line-up."

It may be you.

Now we are getting close to home, aren't we? But don't dodge the issue. Perhaps you *are* the culprit in the case. Be honest now and examine yourself.

Take a good look at your attitudes, your preparation, your prayer life, your fundamental purposes in teaching, your handling of the class. It's just possible that you haven't been as alert and as diligent as you might have been.

Probably all three of these problems have had a hand in contributing to the delinquency of your class. After we have gone more particularly into the case of each, we shall be in a better position to decide to what extent each is at fault. For, having isolated the culprits, we must still get at the causes.

DISCOVER THE CAUSES

CIRCUMSTANCES.

What are some of the causes of discipline problems which stem from circumstances?

Heating and ventilation. Here is a common cause. It's hot and stuffy—the boys and girls are uncomfortable, with that sticky, fidgety feeling that makes them wriggle and squirm—and you have problems. Or, it is cold and clammy—the situation calls forth a warming-up activity for their bodies; they wriggle and squirm—and you have the same problems.

Noise and distractions. Where both eye and ear are drawn away from you to some other focus of interest, there is potential danger. Are your quarters such that the sight, if not the sound, of other activities is shut off? Are you shielded against the intrusion of wandering boys and girls (or adults) who for the moment are not under some other teacher's control?

Uninviting surroundings. Are your quarters drab and uninviting? If so, look out for disrespect. Should we expect the same deportment from a class that meets in the dark, damp church kitchen as that which characterizes the group that has a light, airy, cheery meeting place which they have decorated themselves? Obviously not!

Poor seating. Perhaps the cause lurks in your seating facilities or their arrangement. If the youngsters must sit on pews or chairs which do not permit them to have their feet on the floor, you will have trouble from that source. If you want to know the physical agony that a child must undergo when seated with his legs outstretched, try sitting in that position yourself. You'll squirm too after a few minutes, be sure of that!

Overcrowding. Overcrowding is certain trouble. One child, in his effort to make himself comfortable, jostles his neighbor. There is an immediate retaliation. And the fight is on! Put two boys in one chair and you'll soon have a wrestling match. Put two girls in one chair and they'll soon be giggling.

Weather. It may be the weather. Warm, muggy, damp days are almost always problem days. So are the first inviting springtime days that break the grip of winter and call to youngsters to come out and romp in the sunshine. Then there is the summer season. Other problems are intensified as the thermometer rises.

THE CHILD.

There are many possible causes for the child's misbehavior that stem from himself. Some are immediately discernible; others must be diligently sought out.

Home life. With the modern breakdown of the family has come a failure in the disciplinary training in the home. Undisciplined boys and girls with a faulty home background constitute one of the teacher's most distressing problems. Apparently without any home training in social behavior, they often act more like animals than human beings. And, of course, many of the new children coming into your group will also be without any home training at all in spiritual things.

Physical disabilities. Faulty hearing and poor vision can contribute toward making discipline problems. The child who cannot hear you clearly, or who cannot see you without strain, is easily distracted toward other activities.

Lack of muscular activity. Restlessness, scuffling, jumping up and down are almost always due to excess energy that has not been used up before class time. The child may simply be too full of vigor and you have not provided any avenue of escape for it. The result is that his safety valve is constantly "popping off."

Emotional and mental causes. Is the child mentally backward? Is he a rebel or light-minded? Is he emotionally out of balance? Is the group keyed up because of a previous highly emotional activity, such as an unusually exciting game of tag?

The gang. The gang spirit can work either for good or for ill, depending very largely upon the attitude of the leader and the tact of the teacher. Every group has a leader who is the key to the problem. As the leader goes, so goes the gang.

On the other hand, a twosome may spell trouble for you. Again, it is one who will be the key person in the situation.

Spiritual. In any case the child needs Christ, perhaps as his Saviour, surely as his Saviour and Lord. Unfortunately, his very behavior and the general unruliness of the class, along with your own failure to cope with the situation, tend to keep him in a vicious cycle. He needs Christ to correct his behavior, but his behavior keeps him from getting the message that will bring Christ to him.

Once you have isolated the true causes, you are very close to the cure, and often it will suggest itself. But you aren't quite ready to go into the corresponding cures for many of the causes, nor for the one cure which will help in the great majority of cases. First you will have to examine yourself.

YOU.

Honestly now, have you done your best? Where does

the cause really lie? Aren't you at fault in a great many regards?

Is it in too-late and too-little preparation? It is easy to miss the mark when you shoot over their heads. Has your presentation had prayer, thought and hard work put into it so that it is really interesting? I mean interesting to your class. What interests you doesn't always interest them.

Why is your preparation faulty? Have you no system? Do you follow a study plan? Are you just a bit lazy, preferring rather to watch television than to dig in and do the work necessary for really getting ready to teach your class? Perhaps your ardor and zeal have cooled. Examine your spiritual life for the causes that sap your ministry of its power.

Have you been a "stuffed shirt"? There are two kinds, you know. The one is superior, demanding; the "I'm the master, you are the slave" sort of person. Don't be like that. The other kind—and it may be that you need to develop this quality—is the one whose heart is so great with love that his whole being is permeated with it. You may need to ask the Lord to give you a heart of love so big that you won't be able to button your coat over it. We are speaking figuratively, of course, but seriously.

Study your mannerisms and habits. Be honest with yourself and search out all affectations. Look at yourself through the eyes of the class. Do you have any peculiarities of manner or dress? Things like these can cause you to lose the respect of the class, and when that happens— watch out!

Lack of tact can be a troublemaker. Call a group in which there are twelve-year-old boys "children" regularly, and you'll lose control of them sooner or later. In their own eyes they are not to be classed with the younger "children" and they resent being so addressed. It is a little thing, but important. Experienced workers seldom use the expression "children" in direct address, but rather the more tactful designation, "boys and girls."

Likewise, loss of respect follows failure to maintain order. If you have been ignoring open misbehavior, temporizing with it in the mistaken hope that the condition will improve itself, then you yourself have contributed to the delinquency which you face. Boys and girls do not respect the teacher whom they can intimidate, or whose control of the class they can upset. Listen to people talk of their public schoolteachers of days gone by. Note how high is their regard for the stern disciplinarian who ruled them in their obstreperous days.

APPLY THE CORRECTIVES

What shall we do? Is there no balm in Gilead? Surely there is. Once you have honestly analyzed the situation and discovered the underlying causes, the correctives are not difficult to find.

CIRCUMSTANCES.

There are some circumstances which cannot be changed, of course. But there are many which may be altered, if need be.

Heating and ventilation are subject to control. Have the temperature of the meeting place between 68° and 72° F. Especially avoid having it above this range. Better is it to have a room slightly on the cool side than one that is too warm.

Shut off distractions as far as possible. Screen off the sight of other activities, even if you can't shut out the sound. It will help.

Uninviting quarters may be made attractive if you give yourself to the problem. Too small quarters may be exchanged for larger, or the group may be divided. Several Sunday Schools have even resorted to the practice of holding two Sunday-morning sessions because quarters were inadequate for the crowds who came.

Make whatever changes in seating that may be necessary. If you need seats that are suited to the stage of physical development of your class, get them—somehow. One teacher, when faced with the necessity of getting the feet of her class on the floor, when funds were not available for the purchase of new chairs, designed a splendid substitute which was easily made out of an orange crate. Your seating facilities *can* be changed.

Arrange your class so that there is a minimum of physical contact with one another. The smaller ones will be in front, naturally. Potential troublemakers will be separated as much as possible. And your own position before the class will be such that everyone can see you.

The seasons of the year can't be altered, and nothing can be done about the weather. Since no change is possible here, we must depend on a change of method. For instance, in warm weather take your young charges outdoors for a special meeting. Don't announce it in advance. And when you leave your quarters, don't announce what you are about to do or where you are to go. Have everything planned in advance, and all arrangements made. You will undoubtedly find that there are many distractions outside, and your teaching will not be enhanced, but the change will be good for the class, and its effects will be felt later.

THE CHILD.

There are some things, commonly employed, which are not correctives at all. Scolding, ridicule, and the like seldom help. Let's avoid them.

Praise is a powerful force for good. Use it often. One worker always has at hand a supply of inexpensive award pins of various designs. The moment he sees a youngster disturb in any fashion, he calls another to the front and gives him one of the special awards for *not* doing whatever it is that he has seen. It helps, when not employed so frequently as to spoil the effect.

Another, on occasion, will single out a potential troublemaker, praise him at length for his good conduct of the past few minutes (and sometimes those minutes are very few!). It is simply applying the old proverb about giving a dog a good name.

The writer once did this with unusual and far-reaching effects: The vacation Bible school was assembled for the first time. Seated in the rear was a twelve-year-old boy who had that "certain look" about him. I had never seen him before, knew nothing at all about him, for the school was being conducted in a church I had never visited before.

Calling the lad to the platform at the close of the first song, I asked his name and commended him for his gentlemanly behavior and for his co-operation. He really hadn't had time to be otherwise! Then I gave him an award.

At the close of the session a group of boys and girls came hurrying forward to tell me that I had made a terrible mistake—he was the worst boy, they said, in the entire Sunday School. Hardly had their clamor subsided when the boy's own mother came with the same information. I had made a great blunder, she said, for he was incorrigible.

How could he be otherwise, when he was constantly being told by all that he was so bad? He was merely living up to his reputation. Why should he try to improve his behavior? Probably down deep in his heart he longed for a word of appreciation for his better moments— appreciation that was never forthcoming.

He was a perfect gentleman during the two weeks that followed. Teachers, parents, acquaintances—all marveled at the miracle. I found him at my heels during every unoccupied moment. Best of all, he put his trust in his Saviour before the end of the school. And that summer in the camp which he regularly attended, counselors remarked that the demon of the camp had by some miracle become one of their ideal campers.

Christ the Great Corrector. The supreme corrective for the child is Christ. He can bring a miraculous change in the behavior of the child who receives Him and obeys Him. Search out the leader and diligently seek to win him to the Lord.

Prayer, the imparting of the Word of God, and personal work on your part must never be diminished nor relaxed if the child needs Christ as his Saviour, or if he needs to yield to Him as Lord. You will be surprised at the change the Lord Jesus Christ can bring when He becomes real to a youngster.

But let's consider the child in the group, apart from intimate personal work. Sometimes the corrective is a stern presentation of the character of the Lord as Judge of His people. Try dwelling on such a theme with vigorous emphasis. Don't be afraid to come down to cases and call a spade a spade. The child needs to see his conduct as the Lord sees it.

YOU.

In general, the self-correctives for you are a spiritual life of power, a heart of love, wholehearted application to your task, thorough preparation, together with a proper attitude and approach.

Good behavior stems from respect, respect for the teacher first of all. Then come respect for the class, for the Bible, for God and Christ. Be sure that you merit the respect of your class. You must earn it, for it does not come by your command. Since there can be no respect for the teacher who doesn't have the class under control, suppose we give our attention to the matter of securing, and keeping, the control of your class.

Discipline problems don't just begin when the teacher faces the class. They begin much earlier. Really, in the vast majority of cases, they begin the week before—when the teacher closes the last session. How the teacher spends the time between the close of one week's class and the opening of the next is the most important factor in the problem of discipline.

TRY THIS ONCE!

Do you have a "problem class"? Are you willing to face the facts and make an all-out effort to conduct at least one session without the usual "hullabaloo"? Then give a week to a plan of attack that is very simple and that will work in nine cases out of ten.

PRAYER.

Spend your week in prayer. Come to grips with your problem before the Lord. Let your week be one of constant prayer. Set aside a daily time of prayer during which you will pray along lines suggested below. Pray as you work. If you awaken at night, pray. When you find yourself not praying in unoccupied moments, go to the Lord about the following three things.

Pray about yourself. Be honest, now. How much of your discipline trouble stems from your own failure? Ask the Lord to show you wherein you have failed your class. Put them down in black and white and then look to Him for strength along those lines. Pray for a heart of love toward your class, every member of it, even that irrepressible little hoodlum you are inclined to blame for all your difficulty. Boys and girls respond to true heart affection shown toward them, and just as surely respond adversely to any lack of love that creeps into your attitude. Perhaps this is the root of the matter in your case.

Pray about your class. Have you diligently prayed for their conversion? For their spiritual condition? Ask God to undertake in their behalf. Pursue each youngster with believing prayer, not just once, but again and again. Pray them into the family of God, if they are not definitely known to be saved, and then into a life of growing in grace. If salvation means anything at all, it means a changed life. Prevail in prayer until you can see the change.

Pray for the problem children. In almost every class there is a particularly distressing problem case. You must pray for such a child. But before you do, pray for a heart big enough, and so full of the love of God, that you may love such a child even when he is most difficult. Let the Lord show you how best to deal with each such case. But first, last, and always, pray for the Lord to change that youngster. He can do it—He will do it.

PREPARATION.

Determine that one class session will find you thoroughly prepared. *Thoroughly* is the word. It's a life-and-death matter, this thing of teaching the Word of God. The issues are heaven and hell. Just this once, try a schedule of preparation along the following lines: The idea is that you will be so thoroughly prepared that you'll have material enough to keep every minute of three times your normal allotted time jam packed full of action; so much will you have to do and say that you won't have the time to say "uh" between words to take up the slack, or to try to think up something to do or say next. Just this once, you are going to be *prepared*. After that, if it works for you, you will not need any urging to make it a regular practice.

The Scripture passage. Read it again and again, until you know what it says, who did what, when and where it was done, and who was looking on. Know the passage and its contents. In your mind, after you have read the passage enough to do it, reconstruct the development of the passage until you have it perfectly in mind. Pretty big order, isn't it? But you can do it. Repetition is the key. And it will pay off in your class session. And remember, we only ask you to do it this one time as a special effort. After that you are on your own.

The quarterly and other helps. Now you are ready for your quarterly and whatever helps you may have at hand. You'll be amazed at how helpful they are, now. As someone has said, it is wonderful how much light the Bible throws on the commentaries. By this time, too, you can begin to set up your teaching pattern, either on paper or in your mind. And your quarterly becomes what it is designed to be—a help.

Visualize. After three or four days have passed, spend as much time as you possibly can in imagining yourself teaching the lesson. You don't need to rehearse aloud;

this mental exercise will do just as well, if not a whole lot better. Visualize your gestures, your motions, your characterizations of whatever persons are incidental to the lesson. Actually, if you have followed this plan faithfully up to this point, you will see yourself acting every part before a group of fascinated boys and girls. You are going to plan and prepare to hold the eyes of every youngster. Action and acting will do it!

An object. By this time, too, you are ready to ask yourself this question: What object can I hold before the class when I begin to teach that will arouse their curiosity? Be on the alert for some small object that can somehow be related to the lesson. Here is what you are going to do with it. You are going to stand before your class holding it in your hand. You are not going to talk, at first. Just hold it until you have the eye of every youngster. If one asks, "What's that? What's it for? What are you going to do with it?"—don't answer. Just say, "When everyone is quiet, I'll tell you." Don't demand attention at this point—let curiosity do its work. You'll find that the class will often quiet the whisperers because they are anxious to have their own curiosity satisfied.

Then you are going to begin your lesson. When you have made your start, then, and only then, you will iden-tify your object with some aspect of your lesson. Perhaps you'll promise it, if it is suitable as an award, to the one who shows the most marked improvement in behavior. This will give you an opportunity to award it to your problem child. There is nothing like "giving a dog a good name." It works wonders.

What object? Almost any slightly unusual thing will do, so long as it can be linked to the lesson. Its purpose is to arouse curiosity as you get your lesson under way, that you might have attention. Inattention is the parent of restlessness, and the unwanted offspring of restlessness is misbehavior. Did you ever see a person who was curious about something who wasn't giving his full attention to it? That's the reason for the object.

In today's mail was an air mail letter from Brazil. The envelope with its strange stamp and printing could hold the attention, through curiosity, of a group of boys and girls as the teacher speaks of the letter it contained. From letter to epistle, and then to any one of the New Testament Epistles, is an easy transition. Or, it might be said that the envelope contained good news. One step, and you can speak of the Gospel. You have an introduction, with curiosity-arousing value, to any lesson.

The dime store is a treasure house for those who are seeking objects which might be used to arouse curiosity. But don't start looking until you are well into your lesson preparation. And don't neglect the commonplace. Red yarn in foot-long lengths could be used to begin the story of the Serpent of Brass. In this connection, the writer once invested ten cents in a jointed wooden snake. Though exceptionally lifelike in its movements, it was a poor investment. There was too much curiosity! So we pass this caution on to you—don't be too anxious for something extraordinary!

Fillers. During your week of preparation provide some "fillers" to take up any slack in your timing. Have a Bible verse or two to teach to the early comers, or a blackboard diagram, or even another object which you can use to teach some brief lesson. Then you'll be ready for the early ones and can keep them occupied so that every single youngster is under control from the very moment he enters the class.

Program. If you have a department to provide for, or if your class has its own opening and closing exercises, have your full program planned. Be sure of those "fillers," for you dare not let two consecutive minutes pass without something happening. Don't give your youngsters a single opportunity to take charge!

The idea of all this, you see, is to be equipped to occupy the attention of every child so completely that there will be no time for mischief. You have already discovered, no doubt, that you will have far more "ammunition" than you can ever hope to use, but don't slack off in your purpose to give this plan of attack a one-week trial. Take the full prescription, even though you may feel that much of your week's work will be for nothing. If the plan works, it won't be for nothing; and the plan calls for all that we are presenting to you. It will do two things for you: It will give you enough material to enable you to use to the full all of the time you have, even if the secretary forgets to ring the bell; and it will give you a spirit of confidence and cheerful optimism that is more than half the battle.

ARRANGE A CRISIS

If you have discovered the causes and settled upon the curative forces needed, and have really prepared to meet the situation with all the ammunition you can lay hold of, there is still one thing you need. You need a new beginning. And you must have a crisis to bring it about. Here is what to do.

First of all, have everything in readiness in the light of your analysis of the case. Have a program as interesting as you can make it and as helpful as possible. You can bank on it that if your class is given to chronic misbehavior, you will still have trouble. Very well.

At the first sign of the customary trouble, stop and go into action along these two lines. First, have prayer—aloud. Then as calmly and as positively as you can, without wasting words or raising your voice, talk to the class about the problem. Slowly, and in a low voice, review the entire situation as the Lord must see it. State the issues involved. Show just where it is leading. *Be calm. Be serious. Be positive.* This is first. Close with a simple statement that "we are not going to have it continue; but we are going to have an interesting program and good behavior." Then announce that you and the class are going to pray. Get down on your knees. This is serious business. Then pray. Be definite. Name names and transgressions. Tell the Lord all about the past, the present, and the plans for the future. After you have finished, ask them to pray—you will be surprised.

Then go into your program. You will not finish it, of course. It may be that you will not finish your little prayer meeting.

When the class meets the next week, review the events that led up to this new beginning. Do it briefly, for all you want is a reminder. Then pitch in and give your teaching job all that you've got!

OBSERVE THESE CAUTIONS

Now for a few precautions to fill your tool kit to the very top.

Review. Of course, you'll review the material for your program as often as you can as the week comes to a close. Follow the practice of visualizing yourself conducting the class. Jot a few key words down on a slip of paper as a memory crutch if you need it, but avoid an elaborate outline. Arrange and rearrange until your teaching plan suits you. Review by visualizing until you really don't need your outline. But slip it in your Bible, just in case you may have an opportunity for a last-minute review. Don't use it once your class has begun, unless you absolutely must. Your eyes must be free to catch the eyes of your group.

Early. Leave your quarterly at home (what use would you have for it anyway?), take your Bible, your objects, and get to your class before any member of it does. Begin on memory work as soon as one or two come in.

Perhaps the greatest enemy of good discipline is the tardy teacher. The youngster whose teacher is habitually tardy and therefore cannot keep him occupied from the time he comes in can sometimes get into such a keyed-up state of misconduct that nothing you can do will subdue him. Get there before he does and be ready for him.

A Civil War general, when asked how he won so many battles, said that he "got there firstest with the mostest."

That's what you must do. The teacher should be in complete readiness fifteen minutes before class time at the very latest.

Be firm. Be calm. Be quiet. Be firm in your requirement of good conduct. Public schoolteachers require it; why shouldn't you? Firmness, provided it is reasonable and tempered by a heart of love and a sense of humor, commands respect.

Be calm, no matter what happens. Children have a sixth sense that tells them when they have their teacher irritated and are often merciless after that. Never, under any circumstances, show the slightest irritation or exasperation. Control of your class begins with control of yourself.

Be quiet! A loud voice arouses. A soft voice is quieting. Drop your voice to a whisper occasionally. You will find that wandering attention will be arrested. Try speaking in a whisper when restlessness begins. You will be surprised at how quickly the restless one will give you his attention. He has to be still in order to hear.

Greet with a whisper. If you really mean business— enough to be in your place in advance of the coming of your class, you can set—and keep—the quiet atmosphere which makes for good deportment. As the boys and girls come in, greet them in a whisper. They will react immediately. Seat them quietly, and if you have occasion to speak to them before the group activity begins, do it in a whisper.

Greet each personally. The sweetest sound any person can hear is his own name. See that you know the individual youngsters by name. It will go a long way in commanding their respect. As you greet each one, have a special word for him. This makes possible your doing a bit of spadework with the more difficult children—a word of commendation for this one for last week's good conduct, a word of expectation to this one anticipating his effort to do better.

Permission to speak. Do not allow your boys and girls to speak without permission. It is customary for them to raise their hands for permission to speak in public schools—put the same requirement before them in your class. Always be sure, when you want a wholesale response to a question, to anticipate it by saying "Everyone!" while at the same time making a sweeping gesture to indicate that the entire class, or any member of it, may answer. Otherwise, you will encourage the very thing you want to eliminate.

A military theme. Here is something you can easily put into operation if your class is large. Divide the class into squads with "corporals" or even "generals" in command. Call the roll by having each squad leader report on the attendance of his squad. Grade the squads on their general achievement and suitably recognize the leading squad each week. But be sure that your problem children are evenly distributed through the squads. It may be helpful to make squad commanders of one or two of your trouble-makers, especially if they are leaders.

Let them laugh. The older grade-school boy is a natural humorist, and every youngster loves fun. Consequently, laughter will break out in your class. Don't repress it, or it will break out another time. Rather, let it run its course. Let them get it out of their systems. Then climax it with a pleasant remark of your own and call the class to order again.

Giggling, however, is a different matter. Usually confined to two who share some funny secret, it will seldom run its course. Separate the gigglers at once! Be sure to place them so they cannot easily see each other, or you will still have the giggling as they cast sidelong glances at each other, and it will be in two spots and not just one.

Don't look! Don't see too much. Don't look for difficulty. You can afford to ignore some things, especially if they do not present a distraction to the rest of the class. If you take note of every least departure from perfect attention and behavior, you will get little else accomplished. And you will defeat your purpose.

The grade-school child can listen to you and register what you say while doing two or three other things that give the impression he is not at all receiving your message. So long as he disturbs no one else, let him go.

One of America's most successful children's evangelists refuses to take note of minor disturbances on the part of a single child. "Why should I lose the attention of the rest and direct it toward misbehavior?" she asks. "I have the attention of all but one, and he is probably getting what I am saying."

Look your class in the eye. It is almost hypnotic in its effects. Hold up your object. Wait for attention to come your way. Looking each one squarely in the eye, go into your lesson introduction, and then keep things moving until the very end of the period.

Chapter VIII.

LET'S SING

Children sing! It is as natural for them as breathing. Normal, healthy childhood is a happy, singing childhood. What child is there who in his early years does not love to hear the song that is especially for him?

How early they themselves "sing"! True, it is often more of a monotone than a clear melody. It may be little more than a humming sound. But the child early begins to sing—spontaneously.

Listen to the songs he composes. Everything is grist for his mill—the bedtime song, the radio jingle, his own contribution—all come out in a strangely jumbled message sung to his favorite toy.

Children sing! And this native capacity for song should be developed and used. There is power in music, especially for the very young. Gospel truth which enters the heart on the twin wings of melody and rhythm has entered to stay. It may be but a tiny seed, but it has fallen on good soil and it will take root.

WHY SING?

Why sing, anyway? Why should we be much concerned about the matter—what is the value and place of song in the ministry to the child?

An energy release. First of all, but not foremost, is the value of song as a means of releasing into safe channels the pent-up energy in those energetic bodies. A rousing song service will consume energy which otherwise might be expelled in distracting misbehavior.

An emotional release. The child needs such a safety valve as song, not only on the physical side, but on the emotional as well. The child may bring into the group the emotion of anger, or of grief, or of joy, or of perplexity; and to that extent the group is tinged with that emotion. But whatever his emotions may be, singing helps to restore a proper balance to his emotional make-up. We are creatures of emotion; singing is an emotional experience. It is an emotional tonic. It can be used, therefore, as a medicine for your group's emotional ailments, for of all emotional outlets group singing can be counted as one of the most constructive.

A co-operative activity. Singing with others in a group is a constructive social activity. The boys and girls cooperate in creating something which is enjoyable, entertaining, and edifying. By means of a well-controlled song service it is possible for them to create an atmosphere of fellowship and a sense of oneness which makes possible a common mood. A feeling of having shared a wholesome and satisfying experience is the portion of all those who participate.

A teaching aid. The song service, with its stately hymns and the wealth of truth they contain, its gospel songs and their evangelistic emphasis, its Bible choruses, is a teaching aid not to be overlooked. A well-planned song service can contain as much truth as your lesson, and, because the message is carried on the wings of melody and rhythm to which the youngster is inescapably giving attention, its impression is indelible. Many a heart has been reached with the gospel in the song service.

A preparation for the lesson. Probably we could plunge directly into the teaching task without the preparation that previous group singing can give, but why do it? Better is it to profit by the opportunity to generate a spirit of enthusiasm for the meeting itself, to establish the theme of the hour, and otherwise to lay the groundwork while, at the same time, excess energy is being used up and emotional quirks adjusted.

A musical outlet. Buried deep in every heart, no less so in the heart of the child, lies the longing for adequate musical expression. Not all children have the advantage of owning and receiving instruction in a musical instrument. To them the joining of voice with voice gives a great inward satisfaction of the musical urge. And for those who "cannot carry a tune in a basket" and probably never will be able to do so, the opportunity of singing in the group is a means of vocal expression. The imperfections are blended away.

All this means an interested child, intent on every phase of the program; for the interest gained in one part is automatically turned into the other channels in their turn.

A spiritual need. Song is a spiritual necessity. Ephesians 5:19: "Speaking to yourselves in psalms and hymns and spiritual songs, singing and making melody in your heart to the Lord." Imagine the effect upon yourself if you were to be denied the privilege of lifting up your voice with others in congregational singing. Suppose there were no church hymns, no songs of praise and thanksgiving at the great memorial seasons of the year. Can you think of public worship without singing?

Singing is an act of worship. Unitedly, hearts lift themselves in praise through the old hymns of the church; confession of sin is made; God's mercy, love and grace are grasped. Allegiance, love, and service are pledged.

WHAT SHALL WE SING?

What should boys and girls be taught to sing? There are three categories of words set to music. There are the old hymns of the church, such as "The Church's One Foundation." Then there are the gospel songs of which "The Old Rugged Cross" is a typical specimen. Finally, there is the "chorus," an example of which is "The B-I-B-L-E." Each has its proper function and place in the children's song service.

The hymn. There are those who feel that only the hymns that have stood the test of time should constitute the singing diet of young or old. All else is passed off as less than the best.

Perhaps it will help us to evaluate the worth and place of other forms of song if we understand that the hymn is addressed to God, and is an expression of the heart to Him. That men hear is only incidental. The hymn is praise; it is worship; it is adoration; it is confession; it is supplication and petition. But whatever its content, it is directed to God alone.

Its place in the spiritual training of the child is at once apparent. Not, shall we omit the old hymns but, how can we teach them is the question. They contain the highest expression of worship of which the human soul is capable. By means of them the saved child can be trained in solemn worship.

The gospel song. The gospel song is addressed to men. It is a testimony, or a warning, or a plea to them. In it the gospel may be set forth and a gracious invitation extended to the hearer. As a means of developing an atmosphere of decision it has no equal.

We should not ignore the gospel song with its orderly presentation of truth, its clear presentation of eternal issues. As a teaching tool it surely has a place in our tool kit of materials and methods.

The chorus. Choruses are here to stay! Occasionally used for a long time, now they seem to have taken the forefront in youth meetings and children's gatherings.

Choruses are generally brief, rhythmic, and tuneful, and so are easily learned. Their use appears to be on such great increase that they seem destined to become a permanent institution. Adults have found life and enjoyment added to their song periods when choruses have been interspersed among more conventional songs.

While we hold no respect for the meaningless, jazzy jingles which many so-called gospel choruses are in reality, yet we feel called to defend the chorus that exemplifies better qualities. Modern advertisers have found that a commercialized version of the chorus pays dividends! Just as surely, it can be an aid in getting much of our message across to boys and girls.

Choruses are definitely not hymns. By no stretch of the imagination can many of them be classed as expressions of worship, although some—like "Into My Heart," and "Thank You, Lord, for Saving My Soul"—are addressed to the Deity. But that is not to say that they cannot have a very significant part in bringing boys and girls to a saving knowledge of Christ and then into habits of worship and service.

It has been said that many, if not most, of the choruses available today are not even good music and that injury is done to the musical sensibilities. The author wouldn't know about that, but he is inclined to doubt the latter half of the statement. Musical they may not be, but permanently impressive they surely are.

Bible-verse choruses. There are many very excellent choruses which set to music either the actual text of a Bible verse, or the sense of a text given in Biblical language. Is there anything more impressive than to sing "For God So Loved the World," after having taught John 3:16? There are several excellent musical settings for this golden text of the Bible.

Motion choruses afford a release for physical tension that might otherwise result in a miniature explosion. They may be Bible-verse choruses like "One Door and Only One," or they may be what the writer calls

"Rowdy" choruses, choruses that may be sung with especially vigorous motions and at a great expenditure of energy. A few of them, properly used and with safeguards, to which we refer later, can be a much-needed safety valve on gray days when outdoor activity has been denied the children.

ABOUT YOU

You should be able to step before a group of boys and girls and lead them in a song service. You should be able to teach them a hymn, a song, a new chorus. Yes, you should! What is more—it is within your reach.

"But," you say, "I can't sing." Perhaps not, in a polished, flawless way. But you do sing, don't you, when no one is listening? I thought so! And it was good singing, too, wasn't it? What you really mean is this, that singing before others in the place of leadership is a frightening thing. That is understandable!

But let's examine you—and take note of some qualities you ought to have, which can be developed, in order to round out your children's work in this department.

Voice. Let's begin with your voice. Most of us have been denied the good singing voice—solo voice, that is—that we would desire. But a strong singing voice, while a great asset, is not absolutely essential. A great many are doing good work without it. What is more important is that you cultivate a firm, strong, pleasant speaking voice. You can do that.

You see, in leading your group in singing, you will not be relying so much on your singing as upon your gestures, your facial expressions, your body movements. When the youngsters are singing lustily, you'll be drowned out completely, anyway.

So don't be concerned if you are not a soloist. What you need is enough self-confidence to take charge, and I mean really to take charge, of a song service. Along with that, and it is really the source of poise and self-confidence, is skill—the knowledge of what to do and how to do it. This section will help you to develop that knowledge.

But before we go to the matter of leadin_ songs, teaching them and conducting a song service—skills and methods which are very largely mechanical in character—let us look at some qualities you should cultivate. They will help you, not only in the song service, but in every part of your children's program.

Sincerity. This is first. Try for a manner that is simple and free from any affectation. Your desire should be to give enjoyment to the group in the song service and your manner should mirror your desire. Be yourself, if you are fundamentally a nice, pleasant person. If you are not, then change and after the change—be yourself. Don't pose. Boys and girls are quick to detect and detest insincerity of manner.

Confidence. This quality, if you do not already have it, will come as you discover that you *can* retain attention and interest. Practice makes perfect here—and the way to confidence may sometimes take you through the valley of embarrassing failure and the slough of despond. But don't give up; there is progress for you to make, and you can make it. But it will mean practice and preparation.

Friendliness. Be fond of boys and girls. Be a friend to them. Approach the song service with this feeling. It is surprising how much it will do toward establishing cordial relations between you and your group. Cultivate the quality of friendliness—you need it surely in the song service, and it is indispensable in the lesson for which the song service prepares the way.

Energy. Leading boys and girls in song demands vitality. You dare not be a "slowpoke." Action is a must. Without animation in your leading, you will not accomplish much. Keep in good health and spirits so that there is always a reserve of energy upon which you may draw.

A sense of rhythm is surely needed. Take what you have and by exercise develop it. Your radio can be a good training partner. Turn it to a program of religious music and fall into the tempo and rhythm of each number. Exaggerate the accent. Imagine yourself leading the music —actually direct it, putting all the "lift" you can into it. This is good exercise in cultivating your sense of rhythm.

Joy. This is fun, this thing of leading singing with boys and girls as our congregation. Regard it as just that—fun. It really is a source of pleasure and joy to direct an audience of children in singing. Don't undertake it because you think you can't avoid it, but rather because you expect thereby to derive pleasure for yourself and to give pleasure to others.

Sense of humor. Don't take yourself too seriously. Someone has said that this is the eleventh commandment. Whether it is or not, be a good sport. Know how to laugh at yourself with your boys and girls. The laugh will be "on" you often enough, so you'd better cultivate this very helpful quality. It will get you out of many embarrassing spots.

Humility. Be humble. While it is true that you are the leader, still—be humble. After all, you wouldn't be the leader if the youngsters weren't there to be led. They don't exist for you—you exist for them. Learn to be their love-servant and your leadership will be accepted by them.

Remember that in a certain sense they do not have to sing. There will be many times when they won't feel like singing; they will not be in a singing mood. Neither do they have to like you. You must capture their affection and their co-operation and make them willing to follow you. Arrogant demanding won't accomplish this. Humility does it!

HOW TO LEAD SINGING

Just to stand before a group while a song is being sung is not to lead that song. You feel quite inadequate, out of place in such a situation, don't you? And you are not in control of the situation. But you should be, for if you aren't in control from the very first, you may not be at the last, nor in between.

A SIMPLE METHOD

Let's change all this by a very simple method of leading that you can learn and use as quickly as you can learn a new chorus. But for the first song service, let's plan to put a lot of preparation in it, just the same.

Your posture. A few don'ts first. Don't slouch. Don't make lazy gestures. Don't plant yourself in one spot, in an "I shall not be moved" attitude.

Assume a balanced position, one of poised equilibrium. Let your weight be on the balls of your feet, not on your heels. You must be free of all tension, free to move about and at all times keep your balance and keep to the rhythm of the song.

Your manner. Try to develop an easy, unstrained manner. Gracefulness and graciousness should characterize your bearing while in action.

Avoid quick, nervous movements. They develop a peculiar attitude of nervousness on the part of your audience. They become a bit ill at ease.

Your facial expression is very important. Not necessarily a Cheshire cat grin, but at least a wholesome smile, should be a part of your expression. Folk smile at folk who smile.

Keep your eyes on the group. Look them squarely in the eye. Don't stare at any particular person, but keep your eyes moving over the audience. If you don't—your group will consider you distant and aloof, and will treat you accordingly.

The method. Hand motions are essential to song leading. You must make them, for in them you assert that you are in control. But you can make hand motions that are significant, and through them you can actually lead.

The simplest method of song leadership is to indicate the tone level with the hand, by moving the hand up and down as the tones ascend and descend. Try a simple hymn such as "My Jesus, I Love Thee." Indicate every note in the song by a short stroke with the hand, fingers extended and relaxed. In this way the tempo and rhythm are automatically indicated at the same time. If a tone is sustained over several counts, you can indicate this by moving your hand from side to side in the same rhythm or by moving your hand away from you to the side in a smooth straight line. Then to cut off a hold or sustained note, merely close your fingers with a flick of the wrist in a quick movement.

A little practice and you will feel as if you are controlling the flow of the music and you will have the confidence to go before your class and lead a song.

BEATING TIME

Once you master a few fundamentals, the actual leading of a song and the beating of the time are simplicity itself. For most of us, however, the only way to reach the place of skill and confidence is to hold rigidly at the first to the technical details.

You should master the standard methods of beating time in indicating the different kinds of rhythm. They are not difficult, and you can fix them in your mind in a very short time.

For 2/2 time, for example, the beat is either "down, up—down, up" or "right, left—right, left." For 4/4 time it is "down, left, over to the right, up." For 3/4 time it is simply, "down, right, up."

The down-beat. The down-beat must always fall on an accent. If you will remember this, the rest will be easy. No matter in what position your hand may be, if you have the feel of the rhythm and will bring your hand and arm down on the accented syllable, you will get along.

Not every accent should get the down-beat always, but every down-beat falls on an accent.

Try a well-known hymn—"My Jesus, I Love Thee." What are the accented syllables? While singing the words to ourselves, let's see if we can discover the major accents.

"My *Je*sus I *lo*ve Thee,
I *know* Thou art *mine;*
For *Thee* all the *fol*lies
Of *sin* I re*sign.*"

You finish it. Now try singing it and giving a down-beat, nothing more, on these accented syllables. Easy, isn't it? Actually, that's about all there is to beating time.

But you need to do something with your hand in between down-beats, don't you? Here are the basic patterns for beating the various kinds of time.

For 2/2, sometimes 6/4 or 6/8 time:

For 3/4, sometimes for 3/2, 6/4, 6/8, 9/4, or 9/8 time:

For 4/4, sometimes for 2/2, 2/4, 4/2, 12/4, 12/8 time:

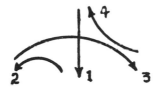

Look at the "signature" at the very beginning of the music to your song. See that fraction? That indicates the time of the song. The top numeral tells us the number of beats in each measure. Having discovered the time, you will next need to experiment to see which basic pattern as given above will be best. The beat to be used is determined by the rhythm and accent of the song. Trial and error does it—just remember that the down-beat falls on the accent.

Perhaps there are extra syllables which ought to be accented, but your basic pattern doesn't have enough motions. Very well, slip the few extra movements that are necessary into the basic pattern as you go along, and you have it.

As you listen to the radio, listen for the accents and come in with the suitable pattern of hand movements. It's good practice.

Vigorous motions. Make your motions vigorous and crisp. Sloppy, floppy motions produce that kind of singing. Keep your hand above the waist, always. And, of course, your motions will be of the hand and arm, not just the flipping of the hand from the wrist.

Don't let your motions skid around all through the air, but make your angles clear cut and positive.

The start and the close. Hold your hand high at the start, ready to swing into the pattern at the first syllable of the song. But suppose the song doesn't begin on an accent! Where shall we begin—what motion shall we use? It is simple—just flip your hand and come in with the down-beat on the second, and accented, syllable.

Hold the hand high also on the last note and on the holds. Then cut off the last note, as well as the holds, by bringing your hand down, clenching your fist at the same time. Watch an experienced song leader do it, and then imitate him.

HOW TO TEACH A SONG

You have a song, a hymn, a chorus that the boys and girls do not know. How shall we go about getting it into their minds that it may be called forth at will? First, some counsel of a general nature:

Approach the work, and it is work, with a spirit of enthusiasm on your own part. Sell yourself on the idea that it can be done readily. This same enthusiastic optimism you should endeavor to pass on to the group. "Well begun is half done" in this case means that your approach anticipates a pleasant and enjoyable success.

Don't take too much for granted. The children do not know the words. They have never heard the melody before. Their musical memories are not developed to any great extent. It is easy to assume that they have memorized when actually they haven't. You must be thorough or you will fail to get your new song across in the time you have for the purpose.

Mistakes will be made. Even your accompanist will make them, for in teaching the new song, you will be breaking it up into small portions. The boys and girls will make mistakes. Try as you will, there will be times when they will fail to comprehend your instructions. Take all the blame yourself. Smile, don't glare, when things go wrong! Avoid sarcasm; it will kill the spirit of endeavor.

On the other hand, try commending every little success. And even when there isn't any success, you can commend effort, can't you? A little commendation here and there goes a long way toward making your group want to finish the task successfully.

Explanation. This comes first. Explain the song. Sum up the message of the verse you plan to teach. Give the sense, not in the exact words of the verse, but in words and expressions similar enough to form a memory link. If there are difficult or unusual words or phrases, tell what they mean; give synonyms or examples.

Explain the music. That is to say, if the tone goes up at the end of one line and down at the end of the next, call attention to it. Point out similar things in the music so that when you come to the actual teaching of it, the pattern which the melody takes will have already been established in their minds.

Repetition. There is no substitute for repetition in teaching anything. The problem is, in the present case, how to get sufficient repetition while at the same time avoiding the disinterestedness of monotony. The answer is to introduce variety in your repetitions. Here's how:

First of all, read the words slowly, a line at a time, giving the explanation referred to above. Then read the verse as a whole.

Now call attention to the pattern of the melody and have the group read the words silently as the piano plays. Make this a game of lip-reading. You form the words in an exaggerated fashion. They read the words from their memories and from your lips in time to the music.

You then should sing the words while the group thinks of the words and hums the tune.

It is time now for the group to sing. You will lead them with exaggerated lip movements. Perhaps it will be necessary for you to take the first half and then the second half of the song if it is too long. If so, put the two halves together finally.

Try this, if the group has not learned the song by this time: Recite the words of each phrase, pausing at each key word that the group may supply it.

How many times have we repeated it by this time? Six, at least. And it hasn't become monotonous.

But suppose the song is difficult and still more repetition is required? Pit the girls against the boys. Have the girls sing it first (they will do it better), then the boys. Finally let both sing together. Three more repetitions, you see!

Review regularly until the song is fixed in their minds. Especially should you review a new song later on in the service when it is first learned, at the close of the session, perhaps.

Illustration. If you can illustrate your new song it will be that much easier to teach. The story of how the song came to be written might be gleaned from one of the several books devoted to such stories. This will help to establish the message, and consequently the words, in their minds.

Use your flannelboard. If you apply yourself, you can find pictures in current magazines which you can use to illustrate successive lines of the new song. Then, too, there are hymn lessons designed for use with the flannelboard. Look through your catalogues.

If no pictures can be found, still you may use this teaching tool. Print the key words of the verse on cardboard, back them with bits of flannel, and place them on the board at the proper time.

Akin to this visual aid is the flash card. It may be a large card upon which you have lettered a key word or pasted a suitable picture. "Flash" them briefly, by turning them in your hands, when you come to the words they stand for.

While discussing this type of visual aid, the slide projector should be mentioned. These are now relatively inexpensive; and a large body of material in the form of slide sets and filmstrips (the latter are quite inexpensive), designed especially for the song service, is available.

Introduce motions, gestures or action to suit the words, where it can be done. The chorus lends itself readily to motions which suggest the thought of the lines. Many songs, likewise, may be set to motions as well as to music. Perhaps the hymn could be better illustrated by one of the other means. Motions to the solemn stately hymn would seem a bit out of place.

Interpretation. There is still this phase of the teaching of the song. After memory by rote and repetition have done their work, try singing the song in such a manner as to interpret it. "This line should be sung softly! This one with vigor! An abrupt cutoff here! Hold this note!" This increases attention, for concentration is called for—they can't interpret the song unless they concentrate on your leadership.

THE SONG SERVICE

Secure the best accompanist it is possible for you to have. The accompanist can make or mar the song service. Go over the songs you have selected, explaining any variations you expect to employ so that she will not be taken by surprise at an unexpected cutoff, for instance. Explain the type of prelude you wish (it is best not to have a prelude for familiar choruses—just a preliminary chord to set the pitch). A few minutes on detail before the service begins will spare you much possible embarrassment later.

But suppose there is no accompanist? Not an ideal situation, is it? But on the other hand, it isn't hopeless. Choose songs with several verses. "In My Father's House" is a good one. Employ choruses with several variant stanzas like "This Little Light of Mine." Look through your chorus books now and note those with simple refrain and extra verses.

Watch this! Let it be understood by the boys and girls that it isn't volume of sound, but sweetness and expression that are desirable. It is possible for them to strain their voices by singing "louder" and "louder"! Volume is desirable, of course, but exercise judgment. There is a limit.

Theme. What is the theme of your lesson? This ought to be the theme of your song service also. Not that every song and chorus must repeat the theme, but surely it should be the dominant thought expressed throughout.

Standard opening and closing. Have a standard opening song. It will help to promote initial attention and order. It will give the group a feeling of settledness at the very outset. Change the opening song from time to time for variety's sake. The closing hymn might well be a standing selection, also.

Special songs. In your tool kit should be birthday songs, prayer choruses, welcome songs for new boys and girls.

Novelties. If the gathering is not too formal in character, a novelty song may be included in your service. By this we mean the use of special emphasis; sharp, sudden contrasts in volume; the exaggerated use of pauses; notes held too long; changes of tempo, and so forth.

One children's worker holds different notes unusually long in each repetition of a chorus. Since the group doesn't know which note it will be, or how long it will be held, they are unusually intent upon his leading.

"Rowdy songs," as we like to call them are both valuable and dangerous. Be sure you can keep them under control and bring the group back to orderliness and quiet. There are some groups that will get out of hand! After an unusually vigorous motion chorus, a race through the final line of some such chorus as "Inright, Outright" (don't race a phrase when it would cheapen the thought to do so), a whistling rendition, or the standing-and-sitting, up-and-down singing of successive phrases of a chorus, bring the group back to quietness by the use of a soft, quieting chorus. "For God So Loved the World" sung in a whisper is excellent in its subduing effects.

Always close the song service on a subdued, rather than an exhilarated or hilarious note. After all, one of its chief purposes is to prepare for the message. Select your song service material with prayer and care, and then so arrange it that it may do its work well.

And remember this: Your boys and girls want to enjoy the service far more than you want them to. They have every right to expect that you will give them enjoyment. Apply yourself to the task with all dedication and devotion, "singing and making melody in your heart to the Lord" (Eph. 5:19).

Chapter IX.

THROUGH THE EYE GATE

The wise teacher will use every legitimate means both to hold attention and to present truth to the pupils. In addition to the appeal to the ear there should be an appeal to the eye—if the pupil remembers but 10 per cent of what he hears while retaining 50 per cent of what he sees, as it is said. Pictures, blackboard, objects, slides, movies, flannelgraph—all appeal to the eye and may be legitimately used to hold the attention, while at the same time imparting truth.

Pictures. Pictures are invaluable. They stimulate the imagination and provide a memory hook upon which the pupil may hang the truth you desire that he retain. Secure a good set of Bible pictures as a part of your chest of tools. When they have been used, put them up on the wall. Use the large Sunday School rolls which illustrate the weekly lesson. Start your own collection of pictures from all sources, clipping and mounting them for future use.

Nor should your collection of pictures be limited to Biblical subjects. Pictures of many different subjects may be employed in your teaching. For example, you might find a picture of two children dressed in fur suits standing in the snow of the far North. This could be used to teach a number of different lessons. If the lesson were on the love of God, the picture would suggest the love that provided their warm clothing. Or if the lesson were on sacrifice, the fact that their clothing could only have been made following the death of an animal could be pointed out.

The blackboard. The blackboard is the everyday tool of the good teacher. Do not draw on it—MARK ON IT. Simple lines are the best. Diagrams are better than finished pictures for your purposes. Draw the fewest possible lines and leave the pupil's imagination to fill in the details.

Objects. Objects appeal to all ages. Small objects, linked definitely to the lesson, may be used at any time. A little scroll, for instance, may be used to illustrate any lesson regarding the history and make-up of the Bible. Larger, more elaborate objects, such as a raised map of Jerusalem, a model of the Temple or of an oriental home, might well be standard equipment for your classroom.

Pictures and objects should be used mainly to arouse curiosity—the first step toward interest, attention, and knowledge. They may be used to teach facts to younger pupils, but the younger the pupil the less power he has to make the transition from the object to the spiritual application where a lesson is drawn from the object. A little girl when asked what she had learned at Sunday School said, "Jesus is a loaf of bread." She couldn't make the transition.

Elaborate object lessons tend to be impractical. Children remember the object, but not the lesson. This, too, is the chief criticism of the use of magic. But not all simple object lessons are effective either. Sometimes they are too simple to hold attention. The child is not curious about the too-familiar or the too-complex.

Slides and moving pictures. Slide projectors and filmstrips have in the past amply demonstrated themselves as teaching instruments. Moving pictures are becoming increasingly available. Used with discretion, they afford an excellent supplement, and add variety to your regular teaching method.

THE FLANNELGRAPH

No modern teaching aid is so versatile as the flannelgraph, and more and more teachers are employing it. Many, however, are not sufficiently acquainted with the medium, the sources of materials and their preparation, and its use, to take advantage of its effectiveness.

To have the eye of a youngster when you are teaching is to have his ear. That is one reason why the wise teacher will use whatever visual aid comes to hand. Truth, entering the eye gate as well as the ear gate, is far more readily recalled than that which enters the ear gate alone. Therein lies the value of the flannelgraph.

Variously designated flannelgraph, vellograph, feltograph, and feltogram, are simple devices enabling the teacher to build a scene or diagram before the eyes of the class by merely placing cut-out pictures against the surface of the board. They adhere to it because they have been prepared by pasting flannel on the reverse side.

The flannelgraph secures the attention at the very outset and, if the story is kept moving and figures appear often, holds it. If the class is told that when you have finished you will ask one of them to tell it and place the figures, you combine hearing, seeing, saying and doing— and we are told that the child remembers 10 per cent of what he hears, 50 per cent of what he sees, 70 per cent of what he says, and 90 per cent of what he does.

Materials.

The flannelboard. If you do not have a flannelboard, one can be easily made, or you may purchase one.

There are various sizes in use. A larger board is to be preferred, for it can be used before small groups in the classroom and large groups in the assembly as well.

If you do not plan to carry your board from place to place, a single piece of Celotex, or any similar "toothy"-surfaced insulating board, makes an ideal board. You may get this at a lumberyard, cut to the size you desire. Since its rough surface will hold flannel-backed figures even more readily than does flannel itself, you need not cover it, but may use it without any further preparation. If you wish a darker surface, a piece of black, gray, or midnight blue flannel thrown over it is all that is needed.

Masonite wallboard is more durable than the lighter-weight fiberboard, but somewhat more costly. If you secure a piece that has one rough surface, you may use that for your working surface; and by painting the smooth side with blackboard slating, you have a handy reversible piece of equipment which is at once a flannelboard and a blackboard.

Should you wish a folding board, easily transported, first secure a large and heavy cardboard carton. Every such carton has one edge sealed with tape. Plan to use this edge for your hinge. Cut out a piece the size you want, making sure the hinge is in the center. Cover one surface with flannel. Of course, you will want to have the flannel on the inside when folded. That is all there is to it!

A table top flannelboard requiring no easel or prop is readily made by taking three sides of a large carton, putting flannel on one of the three sides, and letting the other two sides form a natural triangular base and support.

Inexpensive easels may be purchased, or you may prop up your board on a table. The folding easel is a good investment, for your board is held in all security at a suitable height, and it is easily transported when that becomes necessary. But though an easel is desirable, it is not indispensable—one teacher puts her flannelboard on the piano's music rack!

Backgrounds.

No doubt everyone who has been struck with the idea of employing the flannelgraph as a visual aid has been likewise staggered at the thought of investing in lovely backgrounds. There are some beautiful scenes available. A PLAIN BLACK "THROW CLOTH" FOR A BACKGROUND is just as good as an elaborate scene, and more practical—as far as the boys and girls are concerned. Of course, you would feel better if you had that lovely seaside scene, and another outdoor scene, or a palace interior. But the black background is just as effective and, what's more important, all your figures are in proper perspective with it. It is equally effective as a seaside, a grain field, a palace interior, temple interior, stable interior, or what have you. Lovely backgrounds do not add one thing to your story as far as it concerns the boys and girls who listen to you.

Figures.

If you can secure only a single set of figures, by all means get a set of symbols with which to visualize Bible verses. The symbols are simple and may stand for either a word or a phrase in a Bible verse. Their variety, however, makes it possible for you to have a figure for almost any character and a symbol for almost any need.

The ideal figures for the teacher who wishes to build up a library of flannelgraph materials are those with bold lines and good art work. You need not buy them all—after you have acquired several stories you will discover that you may use figures from this story, and from that one, to illustrate another.

Sunday School rolls—those large colored pictures used in many Sunday School departments—are a fertile source of excellent figures for your flannelgraph. The figures are large, beautifully lithographed in full color, and require only backing with flannel, suede paper, or "flock" wallpaper. From them you may acquire your own library of very striking figures.

In building a library of interchangeable figures, you will find it best to limit yourself to one or two sources, or the effect of several different styles of art work appearing on the board at the same time will detract from your story.

Flannelboard lessons are of two kinds. The first, and most generally used, is that in which a scene is built up on the board as the story unfolds. The scene can be changed with the action of the story by changing the location of the cut-out figures, or by replacing them with others. Its value lies in its attention-getting quality and in its enabling the child to visualize the action of the story by linking the truth you teach with a picture which he files away in his memory storehouse. Since we cannot think apart from mental images, nor exercise the faculty of memory without forming pictures in the mind, its worth as a teaching aid is apparent.

The second type of flannelboard lesson is nothing more than a blackboard diagram adapted to the medium of the flannelboard by drawing the symbols on heavy paper or poster stock, cutting them out and backing them with flannel. It has the same essential visual advantages as the scenic kind with the added advantage of presenting truth in diagrammed form.

One of the most greatly-blessed flannelgraph lessons the writer has ever employed or seen is of this second type. More boys and girls have responded to its message than to any other in his "tool kit." It is a flannelgraph lesson you can make, and use, to the glory of God and the winning of the souls of boys and girls.

A FLANNELGRAPH LESSON YOU CAN MAKE
AND USE

You will need a heart with black flannel on one side, white flannel on the other. You will need also a red flannel cross. These should be large enough to occupy the full surface of your board when used side by side. The cross is easily made out of two flannel strips cut to suitable size. Don't have them too narrow.

In making the heart, first make a pattern out of paper. Paste the pattern to the white flannel and trim the flannel to the edge of the pattern. You now will have a heart having a paper surface with a white flannel back. Paste the paper surface to the black flannel and trim again to complete the heart.

You will need a black crayon and some white cardboard or construction paper, not too heavy. Allowing plenty of space for trimming, for you will cut out each of the following words separately, print these words in letters about an inch and a half high: CHRIST, DEATH, LIFE. In letters somewhat smaller print the following: *Lying,*

Stealing, Swearing, Disobedience, Pride, Unbelief, Evil Thoughts, Foolishness, Deceit, Murder, Wickedness. Cut out each word, rounding the corners, and put a small piece of flannel on the back of each so that it will adhere when placed against the flannelboard.

This object lesson is designed to set forth the truth of Isaiah 53:6: "And the Lord hath laid on him the iniquity of us all." It will drive home the truth of Romans 6:23: "The wages of sin is death." It will show sin's defilement of the heart, the laying of our sins upon Christ and His receiving the wages of sin which is death, the entrance of Christ into the believing heart to give life for death, and the cleansing of the heart of the sinner who receives Him.

In children's campaigns conducted by the writer it is customary to have the boys and girls choose by vote, at the end of the series, the story they want repeated for a special treat. This one has been chosen in almost every case!

You may use this object lesson again and again. Don't be afraid to repeat it; children love the familiar and never grow tired of hearing the stories they like. Use it alone, or at the conclusion of another lesson. You will find it a real soul-winning tool, well worth the time and effort required to prepare it.

THE STORY OF THE HEART AND THE CROSS

(Place on your flannelboard the heart and cross described above, the black surface of the heart showing.)

Boys and girls, even if I had an X-ray machine I couldn't see what you really are inside of yourselves, could I? I can't see your thoughts; I can't see your hearts; but God can. He says in His Word, "Man looketh on the outward appearance, but the Lord looketh on the heart" (I Sam. 16:7). That means that He can see what we are really like inside, whether we are good or bad.

One day the Lord Jesus looked into the heart of man and told what He saw. He said, "For from within, out of the heart of men, proceed evil thoughts, adulteries, fornications, murders, thefts, covetousness, wickedness, deceit, lasciviousness, an evil eye, blasphemy, pride, foolishness" (Mark 7:21-22). Every bad thing we ever did came from our heart, and it left its blackness there.

What does God see in the hearts of the boys and girls here today? Does He see the lies that have been told? If we have told a lie, He sees it, doesn't He? (Place *lying* on the black heart.) What other sins might He see there? (Let the boys and girls name specific sins, and as they mention them put them on the heart. You will have to suggest some which you have printed on cards, but by drawing the youngsters out you will find your printed cards will cover the subject well.)

What other sins might He see there? Yes, He might see *swearing* in the heart. Is it a sin to *steal?* to *swear?* Is it a sin to *disobey?* And *murder* is a sin, isn't it? The Lord Jesus said, too, that hate is as bad as murder. Have you ever let hate blacken your heart? All sorts of *wickedness, deceit, evil thoughts*—these things are sins, and if they are in the heart, God sees them just as clearly as you see these cards that I have put on the heart. The Lord said that *foolishness* is a sin. That means fun in the wrong place. We need to be careful how we conduct ourselves in Bible class, don't we?

What is the most terrible sin of all? No, it isn't murder. It isn't any of these that I have put on this black heart. It is the sin of *unbelief*. Not to believe on the Lord Jesus Christ is the most terrible sin that a boy or girl can commit.

There is a verse in the Bible that tells us how many have sinned. It is Romans 3:23. I'll say it and then you can say it with me: "For all have sinned, and come short of the glory of God." How many have sinned? All. Does that mean that all of us right here have sinned? Yes, it does say just that. And what is the wages of sin? "The wages of sin is death" (Rom. 6:23). (Put DEATH above black heart.)

Can God take such a heart as this, that is black with sin, into heaven? No, of course not. He will not permit sin to be in heaven. And so, the one who has a heart like this, even if it had just one of these sins in it, must stay out of heaven forever and be punished forever.

That's why the Lord Jesus came, that He might cleanse our hearts. (Place CHRIST on cross.) We can't take a single sin back, can we? We can't take back that evil thought, or that disobedience, or that lie. We need someone to be our Saviour who can take our wages of sin and make us clean and give us life. The Bible tells us that God "hath laid on him the iniquity of us all" (Isa. 53:6). He "bare our sins in his own body on the tree" (I Pet. 2:24).

He never had told a *lie*, but He was willing to take the punishment for the ones who had, and God put our sin on Him. (One by one, as you mention them, transfer the sins from the black heart to the red cross.) He had never been guilty of *stealing*, but He wanted to die in the place of the ones who had, and God put it on Him. He took the punishment of our *swearing, disobedience, murder, wickedness, deceit, foolishness, evil thoughts.* "The Lord hath laid on him the iniquity of us all."

Tell me again, what is the wages of sin? Death. (Place DEATH above the cross.) He died in our place, for our sin. He didn't have to do it, but He wanted to because He loved us so much that He didn't want us to miss heaven. So He "bare our sins in his own body on the tree." It meant that He must suffer and die, even though He had never done a wrong thing in all His life.

But, boys and girls, He isn't dead today. He lives! He rose from the dead. And because He is God and has risen from the dead and is alive, He can come into our hearts and live there, if we will let Him come in. He says, "Behold, I stand at the door, and knock: if any man hear my voice, and open the door, I will come in to him" (Rev.

3:20). He wants to come into your heart and cleanse it with His own precious blood. He died for your sin, but He can't forgive your sin and cleanse your heart until you receive Him into your heart as your very own Saviour and Sin-Bearer. (Take CHRIST and tap the heart as you speak.) When we let Him come into our hearts He gives us life in place of death. He takes our death and gives us His life. (Place LIFE above heart.) When we receive Him as Saviour, He makes our hearts white. Do you know how white? White as snow? Whiter than snow! (Ps. 51:7). (Turn heart so that white surface is out and place CHRIST in center.)

Do you think God will take one with such a heart as this into heaven? Yes. His sin is forgiven. The Lord Jesus has cleansed his heart and lives there. He has life, the kind of life for heaven. And it all happens when we believe in Him, receiving Him as Saviour.

Perhaps there is a boy or girl here who has never before today received the Lord Jesus into his or her heart. Will you invite Him to come in right now as we all bow our heads and close our eyes? Perhaps you'd like to hold up your hand to let me know that you are receiving Christ.

USING YOUR VISUAL AIDS

The visual method of teaching serves a double purpose: First, it gives the child a "memory hook" in the form of a picture, diagram, or object, upon which he may "hang" the truth taught in the lesson. Second, it serves to hold the eye, and so the ear, as the teacher teaches. It is the attention-holding value of visual aids with which we are now concerned.

Whether your visual aid is to capture the attention or not is determined very largely by how you use it. In using the flannelboard many teachers place the figures on the board, sometimes before the class assembles, and that is that. You might as well not have them at all!

Watch the demonstrator in the dime store if you wish to know how to hold attention by means of a visual aid. Observe how he uses his visual aid (a bottle of his product and a pencil, perhaps) to keep the eye of the potential customer fastened upon himself as the center of things. See how a quick movement of his visual aids—he puts them down, takes them up, or makes some other motion with them—draws wandering attention back to himself. And all the while he is talking, his eyes upon his audience, never glancing at the objects he is manipulating.

There are three fundamental principles which you should master if your visual aid is to serve its full purpose in your teaching ministry. They are: The Principle of Dexterity, The Principle of Suspense, The Principle of Movement. While these principles govern the use of all visual aids, for the purpose of illustration, we shall limit their application to the use of the flannelgraph.

Dexterity.

Unskillful fumbling as you manipulate objects, pictures, or the figures of your flannelgraph lesson is distracting. It calls attention away from your lesson to your own lack of skill. Try for dexterity so that your presentation is smooth, your handling of the visual aids so subordinated to the truth taught that your class takes no note of your manipulations. Here are several points to observe which will help you in this regard.

(1) Know your story well. Have it down "pat." Know just when to introduce your flannelgraph figures, where to place them, and when to remove them. This calls for practice before you ever face your class. It is a good idea to familiarize yourself with the relation of your figures to your lesson by mentally running through the development of the story while at the same time placing the figures on your board. Tell your story aloud, if you are one of those who can practice in that way.

(2) Have everything in readiness before your class session begins. A chair or table should be placed near the flannelboard so that you can place your figures where they

are near at hand. Stack them in the order in which you wish to pick them up. Some workers place the figures in the back of their Bible, or hold them all in one hand, but this hampers the worker too much. You want to keep your hands free, as much as possible.

(3) Do not stop your story to place your figures on the board. Keep the story moving. Talk all the while. Here is where practice will pay dividends. Keep trying, even though it may be difficult to do at first.

(4) Do not turn your back on your class while placing your figures. Work from one side of the flannelboard, facing your class all the while. This does two things: it keeps your voice directed properly, and not muffled; and it enables you to hold the eyes of the class with your own.

Once again we urge you to prepare thoroughly and practice diligently. This is the way to the dexterity you need.

Suspense.

Curiosity is the mother of attention and suspense is its nurse. Try for suspense. Try this:

Take a single figure at a time from the prearranged stack on the table near your board. Hold it first with the back toward the class. Curiosity will do its work now—they wonder what it looks like on the other side. Do not put it on the board until the last possible moment. If attention lags, let them catch a glimpse of the face of the figure, but only a glimpse. Keep them in suspense.

If curiosity has waned and it is still not time to put it on the board, start to place it—but don't! You will find attention returning.

Do you see now how unwise it is to put your scene on the board before you begin your story? Develop the scene as you tell the story, and then delay that development to the last possible moment.

Movement.

Movement tends to hold attention. Especially does it draw wandering attention back. Use the principle of movement as you teach. Make your flannelboard the focal point, and centralize your movements there.

Walk about as you tell the story, but always return to the board as the center. If attention lags, walk to your board and adjust a figure. Perhaps it doesn't need adjustment, but do it anyway; it is the movement that is important.

Point to this figure and do that, as you teach. A motion is involved, and motions occupy the eye.

All this, you see, is to the end that the eyes of your class may be upon you and what you are doing to the exclusion of all other things. If you have their eyes, you have their ears!

Chapter X.

THE WORD IN THE HEART

There is no service you can render to a child which yields greater dividends than that of helping him to keep the Word of God in his heart. For the unsaved child it is the seed of regeneration. For the believing child, it is food for his growth in grace, and that which keeps him from sin. And in every case, the Word of God truly and understandingly received becomes the source and stay of systematic teaching of the great doctrines of the Bible.

Apart from a direct personal knowledge of the Word of God, how can there be the new birth? How can there be growth in grace? How can there be an understanding of the teaching of the Word?

Early in life the child should be brought to respect the authority of the Word of God. This is first. Then comes, in its time, love for the Word. Both have their fountain-heads in the Word itself, and as the direct declarations of the Word become a part of the knowledge of the growing, learning child, both respect for the authority of the Scriptures and love for them are engendered.

Upon a "thus saith the Lord" let every belief be based, every expectation founded, so that the child may be "ready always to give an answer to every man that asketh [him] a reason of the hope that is in [him] with meekness and fear" (I Pet. 3:15). The child, as much as any adult, needs to know the exact statements of the Word of God as they affect him. It is not enough for the youngster to know that his teacher teaches that the Bible says this or that; nor that his church affirms it; nor even that a certain doctrine or promise is to be found somewhere in the Bible. His knowledge must be specific and particular. He must know what God has said and where it is recorded if his faith is not to falter under the onslaughts of the adversary.

The Holy Spirit can call to mind only that which is in the mind. It is of supreme importance that the child treasure up that which the Spirit can wield in him and through him—the Spirit's own sword. In the inquisitive age of childhood, when memory is at its keenest and when filling the storehouse of the mind is easiest, give every opportunity and encouragement for the child to memorize the Word of God.

From the very first, and along with the memorizing of the Bible verses, the order of the Books of the Bible should be taught. The child should become familiar with the Bible as a book. He should know the divisions into which the 66 Books are classified. Thus he will be able to locate Bible references quickly without leafing through the entire Book or taking recourse to the index.

This cannot be done all at once, perhaps. Some children will be able to memorize quickly the entire list of Books. Others will need to be led a step at a time. Begin with the Books of the Law as a starter, then continue a section at a time. Sword drills, in which verses from a single division are used, are excellent devices both for developing facility in locating verses and for impressing the relative locations of individual Books upon the mind.

Songs about the Books of the Bible are widely used as teaching aids. Used along with memorizing by rote they are helpful. There is this disadvantage, when such songs are used without memory by rote, that some children lean upon the song entirely too much. Unless the transition is made from the song to the unadorned memorizing of the Books, it is doubtful if much is accomplished as far as facility is concerned.

THE MEMORY.

Memories are good—and memories are bad. Some children have the good fortune to be born with retentive memories. Others are less nobly endowed.

Poor memories, properly used, can memorize as well, sometimes better than inherently good ones improperly used. Your task is to use those means and methods which will stimulate the youngster with a less-than-average memory to use what he has with better-than-average efficiency. It is for this that we offer some practical suggestions about the better ways of securing the memorizing of Bible passages.

A five-year-old boy, following an accident, seemed to have lost practically all of his memory faculties. He remembered but two words after a serious fall. For many years he suffered from such a very poor memory that he adopted certain methods to make his poor memory serviceable. That these were successful has been demonstrated by the fact that, despite his handicap, he completed a medical course in later life and became a professor in one of our state universities.

He used but three memory aids. First, he gave close attention to everything he wanted to remember. Second, he thought over to himself what he had read, heard, or seen. And, whenever possible, he talked them over with others. This reinforced his memories. Third, he associated everything new with what he had already stored in his memory. By these three methods the young man with a poor memory became an adult with a memory that his acquaintances considered to be unusual.

In essence, the methods he chose reveal the approach and the principles we must use in the work of hiding God's Word in the hearts of boys and girls.

Mechanical and logical memory. Here memorizing may often fall far short of true learning. There is a mechanical memory which is parrot-like, retaining words and phrases but having no especial concern about meanings. And there is a logical memory which masters and retains the thought as well as its expression.

Beginners and primaries have not reached the level of logical memory and must be drilled again and again on the basis of their mechanical memory. But even here the teacher should give the pupil an idea of the meaning of the passage. Older pupils become increasingly capable of exercising logical memory. By it they learn the central truths of the Bible and classify Bible memory verses accordingly.

TEACHING MEMORY WORK

The strength of memory depends more upon how memorizing is done than on any other thing. What you must do as a teacher is discover the best ways of memorizing and then lead the child in those ways. While it is difficult to improve the memory itself, the ways in which memory work is taught certainly are subject to improvement. Therein lies the secret of success.

Memory must be handled tactfully—brute force will defeat your purpose. A flank attack is better than a frontal assault.

Instead of sandwiching the memory work between the elements of a program to which it bears little or no logical relation, make it an integrated part of a whole. When each lesson has a central theme with every part of the program bearing on that theme, the memory work is far more palatable and much more readily retained.

Correlate the memory work with the other parts of the program. Give special attention to the significant words of the memory passage and choose songs which use them. Employ the same words yourself at every opportunity during the session.

If you are insisting on the memorizing of certain passages which do not readily lend themselves to such an approach, kindle interest by showing their uses, by illustrating them with material which you have employed on other occasions, and by connecting them with passages already learned or with stories already heard.

The old adage that in training a dog the owner must know more than the dog is applicable to your situation as a teacher. You must surely know the passage yourself—

thoroughly. No stumbling, faltering recitation of the verse on your part is permissible. You may read the passage from the Bible, of course—if it is to introduce the verse. But after that you yourself must be out in front leading, not learning.

Approach the memory work as a pleasant experience. The child who thinks that what he has to learn is difficult will take twice as long to memorize it, if he ever does, as he would if he thought it easy. Verses will be remembered easier and longer if he looks upon using his memory as fun rather than drudgery. No child should be allowed to think that this work is hard or irksome, and if you feel that way yourself, you should speedily change your attitude. Assume an attitude of pleasure. It will promote your own efficiency and assist that of the child.

Deepen the initial impression. Vividness of memory is increased when attention is given to but one thing at a time and by going slowly until a vivid and deep impression has been made.

This begins with the selection of the passage. It is obvious that all age levels are not equally capable of memorizing every passage which might be selected. The younger the age, the simpler the text must be. Select the memory work with care, giving attention to the words and the ideas and considering whether they are suited to your group's experience and development. Be sure, too, that the passage, if it is to be the memory work for the day, is suited for use with the lesson story.

Arouse the interest of the child in the verse to be learned. He will not retain much of an impression from that in which he is not interested. Association is the key here. Reach down into his experience for something to which the message of the passage may be linked. Look for interest-arousing side lights on the content of the passage in the light of its setting and the occasion of its first utterance.

You read yesterday's paper. What do you remember of what you read? Probably you remember only the items which attracted your attention—the unusual, the novel, the large advertisements—in short, the things which impressed you. Attention was fixed and you received a more vivid impression, and a deeper one, than you received from those things to which you gave only casual and passing attention.

Arouse the determination to master the memory work. The supreme motive, of course, should be spiritual—to master it for its inherent worth. But sometimes a baser appeal is called for as a first steppingstone. It may be simply the desire for achievement. Or, it may be that the desire for recognition or reward must supply motivation. Whatever may be back of the intention of the child to master the assignment is secondary. The chief thing is that in arousing his determination you have brought him well on the way to successful completion of the project.

When a person tries to remember, his memory works much better than if no positive effort is made. Intention has much to do with retention. It has been found that when a person tries to remember he actually does remember 20 per cent better for a few hours. The same effort improves memory over longer periods of time by as much as 60 per cent.

Now you are ready for the first reading of the passage. Read it with all the expression of which you are capable. Read so that its meaning is as apparent as can be within the limits of expression and emphasis.

Establish understanding of the passage First is the reference. Even with very young children the location of the passage must be established. It is a part of the whole. Always, in your reading or quoting, give the reference first and train the class to do the same at every repetition and review.

Are there unfamiliar or difficult words in the verse? Then deal with them. Discuss them. Give their meanings— or, better yet, draw them out of the class by asking leading questions. Illustrate them briefly. In this way you will anticipate many mistakes. In quoting John 3:16, one little fellow was heard to say "God's only forgotten Son." The teacher had failed to deal with the expression "only begotten." Memory works better when it deals with the meanings back of the words. If the sense does not seem to be clear to the class, do not proceed until it is. Develop the child in the habit of memorizing meanings and he will not need to struggle to recall the words in which they were couched.

Do not take anything for granted. What may seem to the teacher to be understandable words and phrases may, either through her own faulty enunciation or failure to explain and clarify, be stumbling blocks to the child. A young woman named Murphy was the teacher of the kindergarten class. She had taught her class to repeat together the Twenty-third Psalm. As the little voices chorused out, she seemed somewhere to detect a false note. She heard the children one by one, until she came across one youngster who was concluding the Psalm with the words: "Surely good Miss Murphy shall follow me all the days of my life."

Develop the imagery of the passage, making sure it is understood in order that it may highlight the content. If it is not understood it will prevent the grasping of the meaning.

Go back over the passage a phrase at a time (give the phrase yourself and have the class say it with you for needed repetition) and draw from the group comments on each successive phrase. This will serve both as a means of further impressing it upon their memories and as a check on their grasp of the meaning.

Associate it, in part or in the whole, with previous memory verses or stories, the present Bible study, and the pupil's experience. You remember the shape of Italy, but you probably do not remember the shape of Germany. Association did it. When you studied about Italy, its shape was nothing new. It was merely an old-fashioned boot. You had nothing new to remember. What you did was to associate the shape of Italy with an old bit of knowledge you already had stored away.

Not every new thing can be so easily connected with the old. You will need to look for whatever associations you can possibly find. You will thus make the new easier to remember, and you will strengthen the old memories at the same time.

Divide into units. Divide and conquer is the rule. Master each unit separately first. Then combine them in order to master the whole. An excellent exercise is for you to quote the verse, unit by unit after it has been so mastered, pausing at key words and calling upon the class to supply them.

Repeat, repeat, repeat. Repetition cannot be dispensed with, either in learning a passage or in retaining it. A memory is more than doubled in strength if what is to be remembered is repeated three times. Repetition alone, however, is not sufficient. Understanding must accompany it.

Repetition need not be monotonous or boring. "First the girls—now the boys—now all together," and you have three relatively painless repetitions. "Let this group say the first part—now this group the second part—now both together saying the whole verse," and the score is now six repetitions before monotony has done its deadly work.

Use several different teaching aids, if possible, and vary the method of review if you would gain repetition without losing interest and attention.

Use the verse wherever it can be conveniently and aptly related to other material. At such times, when the passage is still relatively new, you will help the class to fix it firmly in mind if you will lead them in reciting the verse then and there. And more than that, it will add significance both to the current material and to the verse itself.

Over-memorize. A verse that is memorized well enough to be remembered tomorrow will not be remembered a week from today unless it is over-memorized or other precautions are taken to keep it from fading. After the class has mastered the memory assignment, memorize it a little more. It is this additional memorizing that will make it permanent.

Make haste. Speed up the memorizing process as much as you can. Haste does not make waste in memory work, but rather the other way round. Efficiency increases with the speed with which the memorizing is done. Consequently, after the class has grasped the meaning, make it "fast and sure" rather than "slow but sure."

Commend effort and recognize achievement. A word of commendation is worth a hundred words of scolding. Look for things to commend, however little the accomplishment. Breathe out optimism and confidence and your class will breathe it in.

Inexpensive awards serve to stimulate effort. Giving an award is not a bribe, neither is it wages. Rather it is the giving of a symbol of recognition. Achievement should be recognized, even to the child, unless it is elaborate or expensive. The best awards are the simple ones—paper symbols cut out of construction paper and strung on cord are almost universally used with success. The best prizes are those that are offered to all on the basis of individual achievement.

This evident recognition stimulates the effort of the one receiving it and inspires the others.

TEACHING AIDS

There is no substitute, of course, for the basic method of teaching by rote. Simple repetition, phrase by phrase, of the verse to be memorized must always form the backbone of teaching memory work. However, there are aids that enhance and support memorizing, and the wise teacher will use them.

Motions. Motions and gestures constitute the simplest of the memory teaching aids. They need not be too apt. Indeed, some will hardly at all suggest the thought. But apt or not, they may serve as hooks to hang the verse up-on. Thus muscular memory and mental memory combine to grasp and hold the thing being memorized.

Take for example, John 3:16: "For God (point up) so loved (arms wide, hands indicating measurement) the world (make circle with arms), that he gave (hand out-stretched, palm up) his only begotten Son (point up), that whosoever (point to self) believeth in him (hand over heart) should not perish (point down), but have everlasting life (point up)."

Try these motions with Romans 10:9: "That if thou (point outward) shalt confess with thy mouth (point to mouth) the Lord Jesus (point up), and shalt believe in thine heart (hand over heart) that God hath raised him from the dead (hands palm up in rising motion), thou (point outward) shalt be saved (point up)."

Songs and choruses. There are many songs and choruses which may be used to lay the groundwork for teaching Bible verses. Some use almost the exact words of Scripture. Others sum up the teaching of the verse.

Unless the chorus uses the exact words of the verse it may be used as an introduction only. However, such an introduction will serve to impress the significant words and the basic meaning of the verse. Thus, much of the work will have already been done when you come to teach the verse itself.

Catechism. Memorizing Bible verses can become doubly worth-while if the question-and-answer method of teaching and review is used. Not only does the question suggest in a measure the answer, but the memory program becomes systematic and constructive.

There are many excellent lists of questions whose answers are given in Bible verses. Since these are usually arranged according to subject or doctrine, the sum of the child's memorizing is a neatly arranged body of truth.

Alphabets. Lists of memory verses beginning with successive letters of the alphabet are easily memorized and retained. In order to compile such an alphabet, it is necessary in many instances to omit the opening words to arrive at a word which begins with the letter desired. So long as the meaning of the verse is not distorted, this is not a disadvantage.

Flash cards. Here is where your collection of pictures of all kinds will prove invaluable. Select a picture which suggests something about the verse. Perhaps it will be its geographical setting, its characters, or it may illustrate the truth it contains. You may even select the picture of an object mentioned in the verse, or several objects, as the case may be. Paste the pictures on a piece of cardboard, printing the reference on the back in large letters.

As the verse is taught, let the picture be in view that it may be impressed on the memory along with the words of the verse. "Flash" the reference at the beginning and at the close of each repetition. When you come to review the verse at later sessions, along with others for which you have made flash cards, you may recite the verses yourself while showing the picture, calling for the reference at the conclusion of each one. Then, to further fix the reference in mind, show the references and call for the class to recite the verses.

Blackboard. Write the verse on the blackboard. Read it to the class pointing to the words as you do so. Have the class read it. Now erase a word here and there. Have the class read it again. Erase a few more words at each reading. The verse will have been memorized by the time you have erased the last word.

As a review, while the verse is still relatively new to the class, write the key words, properly spaced, on the board. Have the class "read" the verse, supplying the balance from memory. Or write the verse on the board, omitting the key words. Let the class supply them as they read.

Flannelboard. Blackboard teaching may be adapted readily to the flannelboard with the added advantage of permanency of your preparation. Once you have prepared a verse, it is always at hand for subsequent use.

On 3 x 5-inch file cards, or any similar piece of light-weight card or heavy paper, letter the words and the reference of the verse. One word to a card is about right, although often two short words may be put on a single card. Make the lines black and bold. Put a small bit of flannel on the back and you are ready to teach the verse.

Place the cards on your flannelboard and proceed in the manner suggested for the blackboard.

For review, an interesting and attention-getting variation is to scramble the cards on the board. Let one of the children rearrange them in their proper order. To make it still more of a game, add an extra word or two not belonging to the verse. Distribute the cards among the class and let them place them on the board in their proper order.

Another interesting method of review is to choose a key word from each division of the verse and scramble the letters of the word. Place the scrambled words one under the other on the board and let the class decipher each word and give the phrase in which it appears.

Too much stress cannot be put upon the use of visual aids in teaching. Experiments have proved that one remembers fifteen per cent more a week after memorizing things that are seen as well as heard.

Memory contests. These are not so much contests in that participating children compete against each other; rather they are contests in which each is pitted against himself. Several child-evangelism ministries have used them with great success. Usually they take the form of lists of passages comprising several hundred verses. Suitable minor awards are made for the completion of the several sections into which the whole list is divided with a major prize for successfully completing the entire program.

REVIEW.

It is a fact that one forgets most rapidly immediately after memorizing. The first day after memorizing, the child (the adult too) will forget more than he will forget in the next thirty days unless his memory is refreshed and reinforced by reviewing the material. Unless there is sufficient review work, this rapid fading of memories is usually disastrous to any permanent acquisition of the Word.

Review must begin immediately. Review the verse during the story as you have occasion to use it. At the very close of the session, review it again.

Do not let the child wait until the next session for review. Encourage him to review on his own account—that very day. If you can secure his co-operation—and your system of recognition and awards will go a long way in that direction—so that he will review new verses within a half-day after the first impression is made, this revival of them will do more than anything else to make them permanent. This is why it is of such importance that sufficient incentive be supplied him.

Encourage the child to recite his verses to his family at home. The knowledge of the Word so used and consequently retained will be all the more useful as well as permanent. Copybooks are an excellent means of reinforcing memory, but better retention will result if the youngster repeats to himself and recites to others the verses to be remembered.

BY HEART

Finally, let us give diligence in this: that the child shall learn his memory work "by heart." While giving much attention to making an impression on the mind, it is easy to fall short of storing the Word in the child's heart. It may get no further than the mind. It is true that the avenue which the Word takes to reach the heart is through the mind; but we must make sure that it reaches its ultimate destination.

Lead the child to appropriate for himself the Word of God which he memorizes. Each verse is for him. Let him treasure them, not alone in the memory of his mind, but in the memory of his heart. The Word is: "Thy word have I hid in mine heart, that I might not sin against thee" (Ps. 119:11).

Chapter XI.

SURRENDER—SUPPLICATION—SERVICE

The child who has received the Lord Jesus as his own personal Saviour and Sin-Bearer is the possessor of new life. It is supernatural life. It is life in heaven. It demands supernatural sustenance, heavenly fare. The child who possesses it must have care and training if he is to enjoy it to the full and if he is to live it abundantly in a world that is hostile to its every manifestation. He must be led step by step in his new life in Christ, just as step by step he is led to maturity in the well-ordered preparation for independent life in the physical world.

The perennial criticism leveled at child evangelism is that it all too often ends with the salvation of the child. There is failure to lead the child beyond the portals of salvation into the fields of service, it is said. Perhaps the criticism is valid. While it is true that much of the evangelistic work done among children apart from the Lord's Day ministry of the church and Sunday School, by the very nature of limitations under which it is done, must so end; it is also true that much may be done through a continuing ministry to the child to bring him along the way of growth in grace.

For the child who is evangelized in a brief, never-to-be-continued contact, the children's evangelist has the sole, but powerful and efficacious, resource of following prayer in the confidence that "he which hath begun a good work . . . will perform it until the day of Jesus Christ" (Phil. 1:6). Do all that can be done is the rule. If your work must end with but an introduction of the child into new life in Christ, rejoice that a miracle has been wrought and that the Word of God declares that such a one is "kept by the power of God through faith unto salvation ready to be revealed in the last time" (I Pet. 1:5).

But there are many with whom thorough work may be done over long periods—let us be sure that the opportunity is not neglected. There are pitfalls ahead of the child, and our failure to establish him in the faith may not only contribute to disaster in his future experience, but will certainly bring judgment upon ourselves. It is a serious thing to cause a child to stumble. Better for him who causes one of the little believing ones to stumble "that a millstone were hanged about his neck, and that he were drowned in the depth of the sea" (Matt. 18:6).

One of the tragedies of the current Christian scene is the neglect of believing parents to lead their children into triumphant, victorious Christian living. The child receives Christ. He becomes acquainted with God's plan of salvation. But once he opens his heart to the Person of that plan, the parents seem to be content if the child is faithful in his attendance at Sunday School and church. It would seem that Christian parents take for granted that the outcome will be satisfactory as long as the child is surrounded by a favorable Christian environment. But the Christian child's growth in the Lord wants not only the suitable environment, but necessary food and exercise, and that at the seasonable time. It is the parents' task first, before it becomes that of some other, to provide all things needful for their child's spiritual nurture, and the provision should be made in the home.

But parents are not alone in their sin of neglect. The faithful-to-the-gospel evangelistic teacher quite o f t e n fails to fulfill his full responsibility toward the child. It is true that in our zeal for winning the young we may often devote ourselves so completely to that phase of our ministry that we neglect to take the child into the regions beyond. The evangelistic emphasis must always be paramount, but not to the exclusion of that which should follow. There must be balance in our work with the young.

The teacher, too, is prone to regard his opportunity to develop the child in his new life in Christ as an ever-present one. After all, we have him before us regularly; there is plenty of time—we think. But it isn't true that tomorrow always comes in this regard. Every day of our neglect intensifies the difficulty of the work. The time is the ever-present now.

Two warnings should be heeded by all who would lead the saved child on into the life of victory and power. The first is this: Remember that the child is a twofold babe in Christ. Do not expect from him the mature judgment and discernment of an adult. The second warning to be heeded is this: Call the child up, do not point him up. Make sure that you are where you would have the child finally arrive.

THE LIFE OF SURRENDER

We have already said that if the child is thoroughly evangelized, he will turn to Christ as Saviour and Friend and yield to Him as Lord and Helper. It is his surrender to the Lordship of Christ that makes possible his growth in grace. Here is the point of failure—that babes in Christ, whether babes in fact or mature adults, knowing Christ as Saviour, are never brought to the point of knowing him as Lord. And it is largely our failure as their evangelists and teachers rather than theirs, for generally there is a willingness at the outset to go all the way, if the way were fully known.

It is the surrendered body the Lord would use. "I beseech you therefore, brethren, by the mercies of God, that ye present your bodies a living sacrifice, holy, acceptable unto God, which is your reasonable service. And be not conformed to this world: but be ye transformed by the renewing of your mind, that ye may prove what is that good, and acceptable, and perfect, will of God" (Rom. 12:1-2). The words are clear and plain. The difficulty is not in understanding that the way to a knowledge of God's will is by way of surrender, but in the obedient yielding.

It is thus that the ministry of the Holy Spirit is brought into play. He would use yielded instruments. It is vital that the child be brought early to an understanding of the necessity of surrender as the means of enabling the omnipotent God to work in and through him.

The initial yielding must result in a continued attitude of dependence upon the Lord if the child is to come to the full stature which is his Christian birthright. He must be taught these things. He must see their reality in your life. Finally, he must experience them for himself.

Can a child surrender knowingly? Can a child receive the Spirit of God in His fullness? Can he live in complete dependence upon his Lord? Yes, more than any newly saved adult. Living as he does so close to heaven and heavenly things, unencumbered by the doubtings and rationalizations of the adult, existing day by day on the basis of trust and dependence, nothing is surer than this: That the saved child may enter into the joy of these things. The adult has difficulty. He cannot "see"; he cannot understand them; but the child goes straight to the fulfillment of his responsibility without wandering in the maze of reason.

Every children's worker who has been faithful to his whole task can cite instance after instance of children who by their simple surrendered lives have given evidence of the reality to them of their Saviour's Lordship. We cite but one.

Karen was only four years of age when she heard the gospel from the lips of her grandmother and opened her heart to the Lord. At once she was brought face to face with the necessity of yielding her whole body, soul, and spirit to Him that she might have His gracious power flowing through her.

From the first, and almost apart from the counsel of the one who was her spiritual instructor, hers was a life lived in complete dependence upon God. To Him she turned in prayer upon waking. She sought His face in prayer times without number during the day. Her delight

in prayer about the most ordinary things of her daily life
was a thing to bring a blush of shame to the cheeks of
more mature Christians. Her witnessing was unusual,
even in the light of the fact that children are the most
diligent of all saints in this regard. Men and women to
whom she spoke were brought under conviction of unbelief; and by the time she had reached the age of six,
there were more stars in her crown for souls won than
will adorn the crowns of most of her elders.

Outstanding? Yes, but God has placed no age limit upon
the reach of His Word in its exhortations and its promised
blessings.

Note the fruit of surrender in the child's Christian life.
Present at once is the tender, helping, guiding influence
of the Spirit of God. Prayer thus becomes real, and guidance positive. He who first gave the Word through those
He inspired is then unrestrained in His longing to teach
that Word.

But there is potential fruit, not to be fully realized
until the later years begin to run their course. What
stalwart men and women of the faith they are whose
whole childhoods have been lived in surrender to Christ!
What men and women of the Word! What a harvest there
is through their efforts!

How shall the surrender of the child to his Lord be
secured? What means shall be used, what methods employed?

First there is the example of your own life. Live before
the child as you would have him live. Let your life be his
immediate example for good. Little can be accomplished
if he does not see in you the practice of your own preaching. If these matters are realities to be known, more than
theories, then know them experientially for yourself and
evidence them before the child.

Teach these things from the pages of the Word. At the
very entrance of the youthful believer into life eternal
you should bring him face to face with God's Word and
its challenge to yieldedness. This is the opportune time.

More than that, as the opportunity presents itself, in the ordinary course of your lessons, teaching should be continued. An occasional brief lesson series on the surrendered life should be included in your teaching program.

Illustrate these things. The Bible is rich in examples, both of yielded servants of God and of the self-willed. Hold them up, the one for emulation, the other for warning. The story method of teaching will be found to be the most effective method of presenting them, for in the story the child enters into what is very near to an actual experience of the choices and decisions of its characters. The lives of the great saints of the centuries abound with incidents which you can employ to bring the weight of illustration as well as example to bear upon the child's need.

Do not forget the influence that others may have. Use the testimonies of others in the class. Draw them out so that their force may be fully felt and encouragement given to those who need it.

The child will early in his Christian experience be concerned about doubtful things. He will come to you with his questions and he should be answered. It is not wise to answer his questions yourself. Let him answer his own question, solve his own problem, come to his own decision. Here is one way to do it:

Have the youngster turn to Romans 14:23: "And he that doubteth is damned if he eat, because he eateth not of faith: for whatsoever is not of faith is sin." Dwell especially on the last clause. Ask questions.

"What is faith?"

"It is believing God."

"Do you believe that God would have you to do this thing?"

"I don't know," will probably be his answer.

"Then you can't do it in faith, can you?"

"No."

"And what is it if you do it?"

He will think this question over. The answer will not always be as quickly forthcoming as the previous ones. But seldom does a Christian child fail to see the principle.

It is better to give this principle than to affirm yourself that this or that is sin. The very fact that he comes to you with the problem of a doubtful thing can be used to show him that the element of faith would be wanting were he to do the thing that is in doubt.

There are other principles, not so general in their character, clearly stated in the Word. Know them and present them to enable the child to solve his problems on the basis of "thus saith the Lord."

THE LIFE OF SUPPLICATION

Surrender is first, then comes supplication. Even adults "know not what we should pray for as we ought" (Rom. 8:26). Surrender opens the way for the Spirit to help us in our infirmity. It is no less true of the child.

If simple faith in the promises of God is a condition of effectual prayer, then the most powerful prayer warriors of the company of saints are to be found among those children who have a well-founded prayer life. One of America's pioneer children's evangelists has said that he valued the prayers of the child above the prayers of the man. Certainly prayer for the child is, as it should be, a real experience of talking to God. How unaffected and unadorned childhood prayers are, and how often answered!

Prayer should loom large in the day-by-day Christian experience of the saved child. He should be taught, not prayers so much, but how to pray. In the process he may need to receive by rote a pattern or form of expression, but his real need lies beyond that in the realm of personal approach to God with his problems and praise.

Prayer should be explained as conversation. It is like a conversation with an earthly parent. The analogy is a strong one; and the child can readily grasp the conception of the child of God similarly going in prayer to his heavenly Father.

Teach the child to pray in Jesus' name. It is only through Him that access to God may be had. It is only by His authority that we have the right to make requests of the God of heaven. Never let the child lose sight of this truth, reiterated so often in His prayer promises. Once isn't enough for this; it must be constantly drilled. Emphasize that it isn't that a prayer should end with a set formula, such as, "In Jesus' name, amen," but that the approach to God is through the Lord Jesus Christ.

Teach the child to pray regularly. "Evening, and morning, and at noon, will I pray" (Ps. 55:17). Teach him to "pray without ceasing" (I Thess. 5:17). Teach him to pray about all things, not only spiritual problems, but the more mundane as well.

Perhaps you will need to begin with audible public prayer. Surely there is no more propitious and impressive time than at the time the child receives Christ. At that time lead him out in audible prayer of thanksgiving for the unspeakable Gift whom he has just received. Such a beginning must surely color his whole future prayer life.

In the group, youngsters should be instructed in the substance and form of prayer step by step. Few children have the ability of expressing themselves well in their early, halting attempts at audible prayer. They need your help.

A good beginning is to call for suggestions for notes of praise. "For what shall we praise the Lord?" Suggest some things, if necessary. Then with bowed heads ask the class in their own words to give audible thanks for those things. It may be that you will feel the need of suggesting the phrasing, perhaps like this: "If I were a boy or girl, I believe I would say something like this: 'Father in heaven, we praise Thee for giving us the Saviour, the Lord Jesus Christ.'"

It is a logical step to go on to the other elements of prayer with the same approach. Someone has suggested the acrostic A-C-T-S—adoration, confession, thanksgiving, supplication—as a guide.

Beginning with the child in the group in such a way and encouraging him step by step, it is not difficult to lead him beyond the single sentence to the more detailed prayer. And in the process he is being taught the structure that he may use in his private prayer life.

There is, of course, the problem of the unanswered prayer of the child. There is great need for extreme caution and studied instruction in the matter of God's express will. The adult has difficulty here—no less the trusting child. The child must be taught not only the mechanics and form of prayer, but the conditions of prayer. A tremendous responsibility rests on you. You, yourself, must know the Bible teaching and know it not only from study but from personal experience. It can be seen, then, how important it is that the prayer life of the child be built solidly on the Word.

Do not neglect the matter of the child's public testimony to answered prayers. It is a means of strengthening his faith as he takes note of, and gives public utterance to, God's faithfulness toward him. And it will be good for you, too! For there is nothing so gratifying to the teacher of children as hearing them recount their requests and the manner of their answer.

These two things—surrender and supplication—in the light of God's Word, are the framework of the child's inner spiritual growth in grace. They must accompany his study of the Word if that study is to be spiritually profitable, and if the third element of his new life in Christ—service—is to be acceptable.

THE LIFE OF SERVICE

So many of the mightily used men and women of God were called to special service as children that it would seem that when God would have a great work done, He begins years before in the heart of a child.

The child can know God's special call. The writer was called to the gospel ministry as a lad in a call so vivid that it has never faded. Wanting the tender, understanding, shepherding care that is the right of every saved child, he rebelled against the call. Years passed before he obeyed —dark years. And when obedience came it was to that childhood call that had not been withdrawn.

But whether or not the child is called to a future special ministry of the gospel, he is surely called to an immediate and "full-time" ministry, and should be so instructed— "full-time," not in the common usage, but in the truest sense. For whether he spends his life preaching the gospel and living by it, or whether he toils at a machine, his service to God knows no limitation in point of time.

Surely, the Word of God teaches that service is in the company of the Lord's people. There is no place here for the rugged individualism that divorces itself from the organized company of the saints. However weak she may be, and ineffectual, the church is still the "house of God, . . . the pillar and ground of the truth" (I Tim. 3:15). To no other institution or organization, no matter how Biblical its underlying philosophy or exalted its ideals, has God entrusted the work of evangelizing the world. It is the work of each individual, yet as one of a company, this thing of serving God.

It is to be deplored that so much fear of the church should have entered into the special evangelistic ministries, the net result of which has been to deprive the church of that to which she has title, the co-ordinated efforts of all saints. To lead the child, by inference, by omission, or by simple neglect, in any other direction than "unto the house of God in company" (Ps. 55:14) is to deny him the fullness of God's provision for him, while dealing a shattering blow to the work of the church in the generations to come.

The goal of the church should be to win and to integrate the child into its worship and work. The destination of the child should be to find his proper place among God's people, there to minister in the gift that God has given.

What is the church? It is both an organism and an organization. There are two sides to the picture of the organization as seen in the Word.

It is the banding together of believers in mutual helpfulness, that the weak may be nourished, the strong inspirited, and the wayward corrected, while all are instructed by God-given servants in the things that make for their growth in grace and their usefulness in the Master's service.

It is also God's great instrument for giving the gospel to the world, the world of men at home, the world of heathen beyond, bringing men everywhere to an acceptance of Christ as Saviour.

In both of these aspects of the church as an organization of God's establishment, the children should come in for their proper share. But, generally, it is not true that the church has taken advantage of this grandest of its opportunities.

The child should not only be permitted, but should be encouraged, to attend the services of the church. Needless to say, the church which he should attend should be that which can and will minister to the needs of its constituency from the unadulterated Word.

Should the child be received into the communion of the church? Should he share in its solemn ordinances? Yes, according to the practices of the particular church. Practice differs.

There are two glaring errors into which we may fall. The one is to discourage it for the time. The other is to encourage it unduly. To deny the privileges and responsibilities of membership in the church to the child is to bring depression of spirit that often leads to the abandonment of the purpose completely.

The conception that the believer is already a member of the body of Christ, a living member of the church as a holy organism, should be taught the child in connection with his entrance into membership in the organization. The idea of church membership is generally held in too low esteem. This needs to be especially guarded against in children. When they see themselves as a part of the body of Christ and are willing to take up their outward responsibilities as a member of the organization, which is that body's tangible expression, they will enter the church with suitable ideas of its importance and will be more likely to become a credit to their calling.

There is, of course, a problem in the child from an unchurched home, who is reached for Christ apart from the stated services of the church. He, too, has the right ultimately to find his place in the church. Parental wishes, even to the point of denying him that place for the time, must be observed. But it is not often that consent cannot be secured if the worker will patiently await the proper time to broach the subject.

A good approach is to secure permission for the child to visit the church and Sunday School. By the time he has visited several times, he is likely to be granted permission to become a member of the Sunday School. Gradually the prejudice, if any, in the home is broken down to the point where the matter of the child's conversion may be intelligently discussed and the propriety of his coming into the fold of the church studied. Many times such an approach has resulted in the winning of the parents as the valuable opportunity for work with them has been grasped.

The child should be taught his responsibility as a witness to Christ. Indeed, this is one of the easiest tasks in the teacher's ministry, for it is natural for the child to bear witness to his Lord.

How shall this be taught? Sanely, of course, in the light of the Spirit's work of guidance and empowering.

It can begin with such simple avenues of expression as the inviting of others to Sunday School or Bible club. A further step is toward a direct witness to his playmates and in his home. Tract distribution affords another excellent step into the service of spreading the gospel.

The final goal will always be that of individual soul-winning in which the child, as he grows in grace and in years, should receive instruction, encouragement and assistance.

The world view must not be lost from sight. The child, while he is a child, may have a definite part in world-wide missions through his small gifts and his efficacious prayers. Teach him that the world is his field. Tell him of the crying need. Inspire him with accounts of the lives of missionaries.

And, finally, pray that every child whom you reach for Christ may be started down the way of surrender and supplication and service, even though you may not be able to guide him personally all the way, to the end that Christ may be made known in His glorious finished work to the teeming multitudes for whom He died.

Chapter XII.

AN HOUR WITH THE CHILDREN

From time to time every teacher or worker with young-sters has occasion to prepare for a special hour with them. It is our purpose now to set forth some principles to guide you in planning for such an hour. Or, if you have the desire to gather boys and girls together regularly for an hour spent in the things of God, perhaps after school, or on Saturday, or after the evening meal, the things we set forth here will be a guide for you.

While the contents of this section center around an hour with the children as an ideal, much that is contained in it will be found to apply to lesser divisions of time. Of course, the principles are also valid in other types of meetings than those mentioned above. Sunday School special days, junior congregations, junior Christian Endeavor meetings—these, too, require special attention in the matter of planning and preparation.

PLAN YOUR PROGRAM

The time spent in planning your program is time well spent. A well-planned program makes for smoothness of execution on your part and for interest on the part of the youngsters. It removes the inattention and rest-lessness that always come when the program drags. Children are sensitive to haphazard planning. They are even allergic to it! They have a sixth sense that tells them when things are not going easily for the teacher. But a smoothly conducted session keeps them so occupied that they become a part of the proceedings and do not have time for inattention and misbehavior.

The first step in planning your program is to set your

sights. What is your objective? What do you want your group to do as a result of the hour? In what direction is their will to be exercised? What decision are they to make? Your objective will ordinarily be set by the lesson which you plan to teach. Study it carefully with a view to establishing your teaching goal. Then plan your program as a plan of attack to achieve your goal with each part making some contribution toward this end.

Decide on a theme to run through the hour. This, too, will come from the leading truth in the lesson to be presented. Select songs and choruses that advance the theme. The memory verse will ordinarily be the theme text of the lesson and to that extent will set the keynote for the entire hour. Let the theme creep into the prayer time and the other parts of the program. By the time you have arrived at the time for decisions, it should be the central focus of thought and action. Later we shall give you some sample programs which will be seen to illustrate this matter of incorporating the theme into every part of the program. Select a theme song from among the more familiar songs and choruses known by the group, and use it at least twice in the course of the hour.

There must be a climax just before the decision time. Having a central theme will make it easy to correlate all parts of the program so that this high point of thought and feeling will come naturally.

If your meetings with the children are to be held over a period of time, it is wise to follow a definite series of lessons. There ought to be some long-range objectives as well as an objective for the day. A series, either of your own planning or already prepared, will be of great value to you in this regard. A series makes possible progressive development of truth. New truth is linked with that which has been previously received, and so there is effective teaching. The "continued story" aspect of a series makes a strong appeal to the boys and girls. It is true that no word of God is devoid of power, and lessons chosen at random will, no doubt, be a blessing; but the systematic, progressive teaching, made possible through a well-balanced course of lessons, is not ordinarily a result of random, haphazard selection of teaching matter.

DIVIDING THE TIME

The Good News Club movement, as represented in the Child Evangelism Fellowship, has found that a very simple division of time is possible. For an hour with grade-school boys and girls, this is the way the time is divided:

Singing
15 minutes
Memory Work and Prayer
15 minutes
Bible Reading and Story
20 minutes
Decision Time and Closing
10 minutes

This, of course, is the over-all division and is meant to be a general guide. An occasional departure is made from it when special interests demand attention from time to time.

Let the teacher and assistant plan together. If you do not have an assistant, get one. Divide the responsibility, alternating as far as it is possible, so that there is a change of leader with each successive program division. If the teacher must take almost everything on the program, at least give the assistant something to do from time to time. It will afford relief and at the same time will develop the assistant as a future leader.

Here is a sample program which the writer uses frequently. It is given that you may see just how much can be done in an hour:

CHORUS: "Give Your Heart to Jesus."
CHORUS: "The Wordless Book Chorus."
CHORUS: Let the group select a favorite or two.

PRAYER TIME: Have the boys and girls mention praise and prayer requests.

CHORUS: "Behold, Behold."

MEMORY VERSE: Isaiah 53:6.

WORDLESS BOOK BIBLE STUDY.

CHORUS: "The Wordless Book Chorus" (yes, again!).

BIBLE STORY: The Brazen Serpent.

INVITATION CHORUS: "Behold, Behold."

CLOSING PRAYER TIME: With youngsters who have responded to invitation taking brief part.

CHORUS: "Inright, Outright" (a good rousing one to go home on).

Notice that while this seems to vary from the division given above, actually the time itself is divided in the same way and 15 minutes are spent in singing, 15 in memory work and prayer, 20 in the story, and 10 in the closing.

THE LAWS OF INTEREST

An hour that interests the children is usually an hour that is profitable, all else being equal. Interest comes before attention, and attention comes before knowledge. To teach children we must hold their attention. That means that they must be kept interested. Be sure that your plan for the hour with the children obeys the following laws which help to insure order, attention and response:

The law of surprise. Never let those agile little minds anticipate your program. Keep out of ruts! From time to time change the order of the elements that make up your program so that the group never knows exactly what is coming next. And, of course, you will plan to make your transition from one thing to the next without announcing that you are doing so. Be well into each successive phase of the program before the youngsters are aware of the fact.

The law of novelty. Use the law of novelty, but don't abuse it. Include in each hour something new or unusual, if at all possible. But don't go astray at this point. Try to do one usual thing in a different way each time. A new way of singing a familiar chorus or of learning a new one—a new way of memorizing Bible verses— even a new way of seating the group—these and many others are not difficult to discover or work out.

The law of variety. Be sure that your program is varied in its content, but don't violate the central theme. Keep to the theme for the day, but avoid "sameness." Monotony of any kind is fatal. Variety is not only the spice of life— it is the spice that brings flavor to your program.

The law of the familiar. Boys and girls love the familiar. Up to the point of satiation they love to sing the same choruses, to listen to the same stories, to do the same interesting things. This makes possible your repeating a story, for example, as a special treat on occasion. Your program will not suffer at all, but will rather be enhanced. Keep this in mind. While striving for surprise, novelty, and variety in each program, do not avoid the familiar things.

The law of restraint. One danger to be avoided is the tendency to give too large a place to those elements of the program that are enthusiastically received. Beware! Interest in them will soon decline if they are used too much. Restraint is the thing that keeps appetites whetted. Don't overdo the things that captivate. Pass on to the next item at the peak of interest, even though the group clamors for more.

The law of participation. Bring the boys and girls into the program as much as possible. Participation is better than presentation. It is more interesting for them to "do" than it is to "watch" or "listen." At every possible point have them doing something—singing, reciting, responding. Even in the story it is wise to ask questions whose answers are apparent and to permit them to answer in unison. Or have them repeat significant phrases, especially from Bible verses you may be emphasizing. Plan your program so that the group is as much a part of it in

its execution as you are. Controlled activity through their
participation will contribute much to interest, attention,
order and good behavior.

Test your program in the light of these laws that
govern interest. If it is weak at any point, concentrate on
strengthening it there.

INTERESTING INCIDENTALS FOR YOUR PROGRAM

If you have difficulty in bringing the group to order
at the beginning of your hour with them, try opening
with salutes. Here are three, any or all of which you may
use:

Salute to the American Flag.
Leader: "Attention!"
Leader: "Hand over heart!"
In unison: "I pledge allegiance to the flag of the United
States of America and to the republic for which it stands,
one nation, under God, indivisible, with liberty and
justice for all."
Sing the first stanza of "America."

Salute to the Christian Flag.
Leader: "Attention!"
Leader: "Hand over heart!"
In unison: "I pledge allegiance to the Christian Flag
and to the Saviour for whose kingdom it stands; one
Saviour, crucified, risen, and coming again, with life
and liberty to all who believe."
Sing the first stanza of "My Jesus, I Love Thee."

Salute to the Bible.
Leader: "Attention!"
Leader: "Hand over heart!"
In unison: "I pledge allegiance to the Bible, God's
Holy Word; I will make it a lamp unto my feet and a
light unto my path; I will hide its words in my heart that
I might not sin against God."

Sing "The B-I-B-L-E."

DRILLS

Bible drills are not only instructive, but they are excellent for controlling activity. Here is an example:

1. Point Bible at forehead and repeat II Timothy 2:15.
2. Point Bible at eyes and repeat Psalm 119:18.
3. Point Bible at heart and repeat Psalm 119:11.
4. Point Bible at feet and repeat Psalm 119:105.
5. Hold Bible aloft and repeat Ephesians 6:17.
6. Sing a suitable chorus, such as "Take It Wherever You Go."

Sword drills are not only exciting, but they also develop facility in locating passages in the Bible. Memorizing of the order of the Book is stimulated and use of the Bible is encouraged. Bibles are essential equipment, of course. Here is how to conduct a Sword drill:

1. Divide the group into two teams and keep score.
2. Let the boys and girls be seated, each one holding his Bible high. (Keep those fingers out of the Psalms!)
3. Give the reference.
4. When the passage is found, the youngster stands with his Bible held open to it. The first to stand reads the verse and a score is counted for his side.
5. If the children are more or less unfamiliar with the Bible, give references in limited sections at first.

Introduce a slogan frequently. "God said it, Jesus did it, I believe it, that settles it" is a good example, but you can produce others just as good—even better.

A five-finger exercise such as this one will help to bring the class to attention if attention has wandered: 1. God loved. 2. I sinned. 3. Christ died. 4. I believe. 5. I live.

IT'S FUN TO REVIEW THIS WAY—

Some years ago during the course of a daily vacation Bible school the intermediate department became unusually difficult. The quarters were overcrowded, the weather was hot and steamy with rain every day preventing outdoor relaxation, and the intermediates seemed to be particularly uninterested in the Old Testament history being taught. Recourse was taken to the game known as Bible Baseball. After introducing the game it was announced that the final half-hour of the morning would be devoted to it, with all questions to be taken from the D.V.B.S. lessons.

The result was revolutionary. All discipline problems ended. Interest ran high throughout every lesson. Best of all, the boys and girls absorbed the material being taught so completely that it was altogether astounding.

The game is simple, but as exciting as any athletic event can be.

The Rules:

1. The game may be played with any number on each team. Teams may be made up on any suitable basis, boys against girls, "choose up," or any other division.

2. Lay out a baseball diamond if open space is available. If not, use the four corners of the room as bases.

3. Prepare two sheets of Bible questions, preferably based on previous lessons. The umpire may use any means to decide which team shall have the choice of sheets. The other team takes the remaining list.

4. Each team has a regular batting order with batters coming to the plate in rotation.

5. The pitcher selects a question and reads it. If the batter fails to answer or if he answers incorrectly, he is "out."

6. If the batter answers correctly, he moves to first base. There are no "balls" or "strikes."

7. An interesting and exciting variation is to let the members of each team "pitch" in rotation just as they "bat." Let each compose his own question, apart from any prepared lists. How they will pay attention to the lessons, looking for good questions to have ready when the game is played!

8. Runners advance on the bases just as they do in real baseball. However, they can advance but one base at a

time. Scoring is as in the real game, a run for each man who is advanced across home plate.

9. The teacher should umpire, of course.

10. Each side is allowed three "outs" before being retired. Those who are "left on base" do not count in the scoring.

11. It is a good idea to place a 15- or 30-second time limit on the questions. If the batter does not give the correct answer within the allotted time, he is "out."

12. If the players are allowed to ask questions of their own arranging, a good rule to have is that the pitcher must be able to answer his own question. If he can't, the batter should be "walked."

Try It!

Try this game. The first time your youngsters play it they may find it a little strange, but it won't be long until they take over. Don't limit it just to questions of fact; use it to promote Scripture memorizing. You will find boys and girls memorizing at home in order that they may have some "fast balls" to put over.

Once the group is acquainted with the game, you may use it to promote special, intensified study. All you need do is to give advance warning that the next time the game is played its questions must be limited to a certain chapter, or a certain theme. Watch them dig in for some real study.

The Secret

The secret of the success of Bible Baseball as a teaching aid is that it introduces the elements of suspense and excitement to what can be, and usually is, rather routine drudgery of mind. There is good reason for special interest; and what people are interested in they give attention to. Interest is the mother of attention, and attention is the mother of learning. Bible Baseball gets learning's grandmother into the teaching picture.

In the instance cited at the beginning the writer was amazed at the wealth of facts that his intermediates had stored away in their minds. The lesson material dealt with the Exodus, with the chief emphasis upon the typical teaching of the Tabernacle. The questions asked in the daily review games were a revelation of how much information and application could be packed into an intermediate so painlessly. Nor did they get it all from the daily lessons! They soon began to inquire about the advance assignments in order that they might study at home.

Warning!

One warning—don't let the individual games run too long. Too much of anything will dull the appetite. Better set a time limit of fifteen, twenty or thirty minutes and end the game on time. This will keep interest whetted, and it will prevent the game from getting out of hand. After all, it is a game, although a good one with a good purpose in view; but back of the game is the Word, and that is the consideration not to be lost from view.

At the close of each game have prayer together. Though excitement may run high, do not end on that note. There will be no carry-over of feeling if the group gathers around the throne of grace for a moment of quiet reverence.

CONTESTS, PRIZES AND AWARDS

Nothing is quite as stimulating as a good contest, rightly conducted. However, there are contests and contests. Let yours be simple. The elaborate kind usually bogs down of its own weight.

For a simple contest that can become quite exciting, divide the class into two groups. Give points (they cost nothing!) for behavior, effort, bringing visitors, etc. Extra points may be given from time to time for special things, or for stimulating endeavor at some weak point. A simple treat at the close, with the losers invited at the last minute by the winners (you'll suggest it, of course), is a suitable climax. Don't run any contest very long. Four weeks is enough, if you meet weekly.

The best contest is that in which each individual has a chance to receive an award. The disposition to seek praise is natural, and praise is an incentive to do well. We recognize this when we give awards, recognitions, or honor certificates. Those who deserve praise and recognition should surely receive it. Every contest ought to have this element of individual recognition in it. Let the individual awards be inexpensive and keep the treat as simple as possible.

TRY A QUIZ!

Are you looking for something that will stimulate lagging attendance and diminishing interest? Try a quiz. Boys and girls are especially fond of them.

Announce to your group that in two (or three, or four) weeks you will have a quiz. Then you can begin to emphasize your points as you teach by saying something like this: "Remember that, because it might be one of the quiz questions: Who were the two faithful spies that returned from Canaan with a good report?" It is always wise to limit the questions to the material you will be studying between your announcement and the quiz itself. You will discover your class displaying a new interest in the lessons.

If your class is large and has a diversity of ages, you will need to put on a youngsters' and later an oldsters' quiz. Ask, "How many of you aged six to eight would like to take part?" If there are more than five or six, pass out slips of paper. On five or six (according to the number you want to participate) you will have placed some identifying marks. The children drawing the slips so marked are the ones to participate in the quiz.

If the group is evenly aged, and of uniform intelligence, you will not need to limit participation to youngsters or oldsters. But in no event should more than six take part if you want your quiz to be fast-moving. Have six chairs facing the class. These are for your "experts." Have the

questions written out. Be sure they are clear, having
been well thought out and clearly stated, and capable of
a definite answer.

Have an assistant to sit facing the quiz contestants. It
will be his task to keep score. Score 10 points for perfect
answers, proportionately less for partial answers.

Cautions!

Be very, very sure not to allow too much time for the
answers. This could ruin your quiz. The count of ten, and
let it be a snappy count, is enough. This will keep the
interest from dragging. The entire success of the quiz
may hinge on just this point.

If a child fails to give the correct answer, do not pass
the same question on to the quiz participants. Put it up
to the class. This gives them a part in the activities.

It is a good thing to let only those who have been present at all the previous sessions compete. Otherwise they
may say, "I wasn't here that day!" The result is that
you must either eliminate the child, unfairly he thinks,
or else throw your question sequence entirely out for his
sake.

Quiz Questions

It is absolutely essential to have your questions written
out. It takes time, but it is time well spent. Have variety
in the questions. Prepare several sets, with each set presenting a new approach or a different method of questioning. Here are some examples:

General Review Questions. Why did the Children of
Israel go down to Egypt? How many of them went to
Egypt? Who was the deliverer God raised up?

True or False Questions—(answer in one word). The
Children of Israel were kindly treated by the taskmasters
in Egypt (false). The baby Moses was hidden among the
flags (true). Moses lived in the palace of the Pharaohs
for 45 years (false).

Complete the Verse Questions. Without the shedding
of ———— is no ————. I am the ————: by me if any

——— enter ——— he shall be ———. All have ———
and come ——— of the ——— of ———.

Correct This Statement. There were seven hundred
Children of Israel that went down to Egypt. There were
twenty-four tribes of the Children of Israel. The roof of
the Tabernacle was solid gold.

Salvation Questions. (Always include a set.) Why did
the Lord Jesus die on the cross? What must I do to be
saved? Can I be saved by doing good, or by being good?

Guess Who. "I'm a little girl watching my baby brother.
Who am I?" "I am angry and dash two stone tablets
to the ground. Who am I?" "I am Moses' and Miriam's
brother, and I am the high priest. Who am I?"

Always have extra questions on hand in case there is
a tie. These should be a bit more difficult in order to bring
the quiz to an end in quick order if the tie needs to be
broken.

Do not be surprised if the boys and girls in the audience
get a bit restless. This is because they are not in the lime-
light, and for that reason the time allowed for answering
the questions must be very brief. For this reason, too,
unanswered questions should be referred to the boys and
girls in the audience.

Explain that the audience *must not* assist in the quiz
by helping with the answers. There must be no coaching
or prompting on your part, either. You must be absolutely
impartial, and it is hard to do so if you once give even
a little hint to one of the contestants.

Make it a hard and fast rule that the first answer the
contestant gives is the one that counts.

Either keep to the rules and limits, or have none.

At the conclusion of the questioning, have the scores
read out, and the one having the highest score should be
declared the winner. In case of a tie, have the rest take
their seats in the audience and go on with the extra questions. If you wish to terminate the quiz rapidly and your
questions are not doing it, try calling for Scripture passages. This will usually bring about a speedy end.

Give the winner an award, if possible, and let the children applaud.

The class will want another quiz the very next week, but stand your ground and let them wait for several weeks. In the meantime they will be pointing toward the quiz, and as you teach they will be alert lest they miss something important. You will be amazed at the way their interest will mount up.

YOUR FIRST CHILD-EVANGELISM CLASS

Now is the time to start that child-evangelism class that you have wanted to have. Or, if you have had a class in other years, now is the time to start again. Here are some hints and helps for your first meeting:

Invitations. As soon as you know the day and the place of your class, secure printed invitations. A few dollars spent with a commercial printer will be a good investment. The "ticket" type of invitation has been of especial value in advertising these Bible-club meetings. However, there are available printed cards and blotters which need only to have the time and place filled in by hand. Whatever kind of invitation is secured or prepared, be sure that you have a sufficient quantity of them.

Go to the vicinity of the nearest school from time to time during the week just prior to the opening of your class and give out your invitations. Don't go on the school grounds; you must have special permission to do that. *You need no permission* to distribute your tickets to passers-by from the sidewalk adjacent to the school ground.

On the day of the class it is a good thing to go to the vicinity of the school at noon to distribute the balance of your invitations and then again as school is dismissed in the afternoon. The afternoon visit serves as a reminder, something that is really needed at first, for until habit works in your behalf the day and hour of your meeting will be readily forgotten.

Prepare. It goes without saying that you must be thoroughly prepared for your first session, better prepared than for any other that shall follow. Study your lesson well. Read it over every day. Talk it over with yourself. Nothing will give you more poise and self-assurance than to be thoroughly prepared. And don't think that the respect and interest of the child are not directly affected by your mastery of your material—they are!

Program. Until you no longer need it, make a program for each session. If you have a pianist to assist, see that she has a copy of the program with the location of songs and choruses supplied. It is distracting to wait while the pianist searches for the music to the song you and your class are waiting to sing. See that she has the necessary information before her.

When the hour comes. Do we need to tell you that you should have everything in readiness at least fifteen minutes before the class is to begin? Have your equipment set, the chairs arranged, materials organized, chorus books on the piano—have everything in its place.

Be enthusiastic and cordial as you greet the children, some of whom will probably be a bit shy. Make them feel at home. Make them feel important and glad that they came. Some teachers whisper all greetings and conversation at the door and find that it tends to subdue the group. They unconsciously assume a hushed attitude. Try it sometime.

Seating. If the class is not too large, arrange seats in a circle, selecting for the teacher a place where all can easily see. Never permit two children (boys especially) to occupy a single chair unless it is absolutely unavoidable. Just as soon as you do, you will have a case of giggling or wrestling before the class is over.

Get the names and addresses of the children as coats and hats are being removed. Do not take the time for this once the class is seated and eager to get under way. If it hasn't been completed, let it wait until the end of the class—even at the risk of not getting the information.

Many teachers make the mistake of delaying the start of the program until all desirable information is recorded. It is dangerous! Little Billy is interested only in his own name, and when he has given it he starts looking around for mischief, which he usually finds. When the time to begin comes—begin, regardless!

Tell the youngsters to put whatever they have in their hands, under their chairs. Even an innocent pencil can prove to be a great distraction. Bill points it at Jack. Jack grabs for it. Bill jerks it back with such an effort that he falls to the floor—and you have a situation!

Songs. Select simple choruses for your first session. "I Will Make You Fishers of Men," "Everything's All Right in My Father's House," "This Little Light of Mine" are excellent because they are easy and the additional verses add variety. Do not ask whether they know the song or not, just pitch in and teach it as if none knew it.

Bible Drill. Hold up your Bible and ask, "What is this?" Take a few minutes for general information about the Bible, such as: Author, other names for it, number of divisions, etc. Later you may have a drill in which the youngsters can compete against each other, but the first day probably will be so full that you can't do more than make a brief introduction. Close this part of your program with a Bible chorus, such as "The B-I-B-L-E," or, if time permits, the first verse of the "Books of the Bible Song."

Prayer. Ask this question: "Did you know that we can talk to God, the Author of the Bible, and that He will hear and answer when we talk to Him? We are going to bow our heads, shut our eyes, and fold our hands as we talk to God." Pray very briefly, in simple words and short sentences.

Memory Work. Keep verses simple at first, especially if there are many of the younger children in the group. Do not spend too much time on the memory work at this first session. Have the boys say it once, then the girls. Avoid too much individual recitation—the rest of the class can get out of hand if you do.

The Story. This is the big moment! "Everybody wiggle —get comfortable!" Wait for quiet and attention. "Once upon a time—" and you're off! Be dramatic no matter how foolish you feel. Act it out! Be brief; fifteen to twenty minutes is enough at this first session. And don't neglect to tell the group how to be saved. That's your purpose.

SOME HINTS AND HELPS

A well-planned program is half the battle; but after all, it must be successfully executed if it is to bring its proper harvest. Here are some hints and helps that may be of value to you as you conduct your hour with the boys and girls.

Set a fast pace. If there is anything that is sudden death to interest, it is a slow tempo. Let things slow down, and interest lags at once. It is necessary, therefore, to keep things humming. Avoid delays as you would the plague. For instance, if someone is coming to the center of the platform or the front of the group, don't just wait—sing a chorus, repeat in unison a Bible verse. You can't afford to let two consecutive minutes pass without something being done under your control. If you do, there is more than just a likelihood that little Billy sitting in the third row will take charge of his small section!

Change your pace. Setting a fast pace, doesn't mean that you must do everything at top speed, that songs are to be sung at top speed, and that sort of thing. It means that your program must *move.* There are times when you must do something in a slower tempo and a lower key. It is here that "change of pace" comes in. After a fast, rousing, more-or-less "rowdy" chorus, try a soft, low, slow one. If you call for a few vigorous responses from the group, let them whisper one. Loud—soft; fast—slow; humorous—serious; bring contrast into your program. Change your pace!

You will find this principle invaluable as a means of recapturing wandering attention. As you are telling your story, as an example, you may notice that there is some restlessness. Perhaps you've been talking in a monotone without your noticing it. Whisper a sentence or two. You will be surprised at how quickly heads snap up and eyes come your way. It is electric in its effects. Try it.

Start, stop on time; do nothing unnecessary. When the time comes to begin—begin! Why wait, if there is someone there? If you wait a minute this week, you may find it necessary to wait two minutes next week, and there is no end. If you are prompt, your youngsters will learn to be prompt. Yield to them, and the inch becomes a mile, or rather, the minute becomes an hour.

And when you begin—just begin. Don't waste words telling the boys and girls that it's time to begin. They'll know it, if you just launch into your program. Avoid unnecessary announcements, like: "Now, boys and girls, it's time for our Bible memory verse"; rather, plunge into the teaching of the verse. They'll soon find out that the time for that particular feature is at hand. Do the same with your story. You will find that you will have far better attention. Don't give those keen little minds a single opportunity to anticipate your program.

Beginning on time really means that you will be on hand much earlier. Have all your last-minute preparations out of the way fifteen minutes before the hour. This means that you will have checked the room temperature and adjusted the ventilation; seating will have been arranged; all materials to be used will have been placed where you can reach them. Then you can begin to occupy the attention of the early-comers with memory reviews, a brief object lesson, or whatever you have chosen to fill up before-session minutes. And when it's time to begin—begin!

Don't stretch! Don't try to stretch fifty minutes of program to cover an hour when you suddenly discover that your program is to run short. It would be better to have a "filler" always ready for such a situation. If not, end your program at the fifty-minute mark. If your program is apparently going to run longer than your hour, or hour and a quarter—whatever is your normal time span —eliminate something.

This principle applies to your story, too. Let it be only as long as it will hold the interest. Why tell it, if it isn't getting across? And if it doesn't get across to the boys and girls, examine yourself and your methods to see why. And let that be a lesson to you! The average age of your group will govern the length of your story. Twenty minutes is about average—less for younger groups, more for older groups. I have seen groups held spellbound for fifty minutes by a dynamic storyteller. You and I, perhaps, will do well to limit ourselves to twenty or twenty-five minutes.

Be enthusiastic. Whatever you do, do it with all the zest at your control. Be enthusiastic! Yes, even if there are only two present. Don't let anything dull your enthusiasm. Remember that nothing is more contagious than depression of spirit, unless it is a bright, sprightly attitude before your audience. The old man who told the young preacher that his sermon was all right but that he didn't deliver it with "enthusi-enough-asm" had the right slant.

Put yourself into whatever you do. If you don't feel very enthusiastic, at least act as if you are. Strangely enough, you'll soon find that your simulated enthusiasm has become the real thing! If you don't believe it, just try it.

Love. Finally, be interested in your group. Pack more love, affection, and kindness into your program than they have ever witnessed before. Love answers to love. Nothing is more conducive to interest and attention than this very thing. With all the mechanics of leading a group of youngsters, this is the real secret—you must have a heart of love that yearns for them, that longs to see them won for Christ, that hungers after their development in Him.

Chapter XIII.

A GREAT DOOR AND EFFECTUAL

When our Lord gave the marching orders for His forces in the gospel age, He gave them in a way that included the reaching of every person in the world. "Go ye," He said, "into all the world, and preach the gospel to every creature." Surely He meant that children, too, were to be told that He had died for sin, had been buried, had risen again that they might have a Saviour who would be able and willing to come into their hearts to cleanse them and live in them. Elsewhere in the New Testament there has been laid down an actual program that by positive direction points us to the children by specific command.

THE HOME

Christians are to evangelize their own children. Ephesians 6:4: "And, ye fathers, provoke not your children to wrath: but bring them up in the nurture and admonition of the Lord." This is the responsibility of the father. If he doesn't do it, it becomes the mother's task. Pity the Christian father who cannot take his child and point him to Calvary while he is still a child! When we see that this is the duty of the Christian parent first, before it becomes that of the pastor or Sunday School teacher, and when we as Christian parents fulfill our ministry in our own family circles, we shall have taken a great step forward in stemming the decline in all the effectiveness of our united testimony.

God has placed within us the physical power to reproduce our kind. With this power He has given sufficient native intelligence for us to educate our young to live in this material world. The facts in the case argue for themselves. It would be a sad world indeed if it were not so. Is it less true of the spiritual realm? If He has given us the things necessary to train our children to become strong, mature men and women, shall He not also give us the things necessary to bring them into the possession of spiritual life and to train them in the life of the Spirit? Therefore, let believing parents awaken to their accountability in this regard, build again the family altar that has crumbled in disuse, and enjoy the rare privilege of themselves bringing their little ones to Christ.

The program of God's ingathering begins within the four walls of the Christian home. The boys and girls of believing homes have every right to hear the gospel from the parents who brought them into the world. They have every right to find their Saviour through their parents' personal ministry to them. Every Christian husband and father has a flock of which he is the pastor, and for which he shall someday give account. Oh! the pity that sons and daughters of believing parents should go into adolescence without a personal experience of Christ in their hearts!

The one place where boys and girls have the right first to receive Christ has very largely neglected to fulfill its basic responsibility toward them. That which was designed to be the bulwark against unbelief—the Christian family circle—is fast becoming the spawning ground for willful unbelief. The personal salvation of sons and daughters has been neglected in the home and left to other and often disinterested hands.

Why Should It Be?

Why have so many Christian parents left the evangelizing of their children to others? Is it because parents have failed to appreciate the growing power of inborn sin? Is it because of a Pollyanna attitude toward childhood sin? Is there ignorance of the Word of God which says that the "wicked are estranged from the womb: they go astray as soon as they be born, speaking lies"? (Ps. 58:3).

Is it because they have failed to note the naturalness of child conversion as it is presented in the Word and seen in experience? Have they never considered the seriousness of neglecting the boys and girls, according to Matthew 18:6-10? Why have they never claimed the promise of Matthew 18:14, a promise which any parent can claim before a loving heavenly Father, and knowingly pray according to His will? Do they not realize that the boy or girl who is not positively led to Christ will as surely, and as readily, be led away from Him?

The Family Circle.

Christian homes are our most powerful weapons against world unbelief. Here the sons and daughters of believers may be nurtured in a deeply-spiritual atmosphere, taught in the richness of the Word of God, established in the faith, that they may face Satan and his emissaries unashamed and unafraid—if the home is Christian in the fullest sense.

But the foundations of our family life need pointing up. The Godliness of parents must be manifested in daily living. The family altar, with the head of the family ministering the Word of God and leading his little flock to the fountain springs of mercy daily, must again become the power of every Christian family. The responsibility of parenthood in all its spiritual requirements must be taken up and parents must be found in supplication before God and in entreaty before their young, that their boys and girls may be privileged to find Christ within the circle of the family and there be established in the Word of God.

THE SUNDAY SCHOOL

A second wall of defense, the organized forces of the church, likewise has begun to crumble away. The Sunday School ought to be a major out-reaching evangelistic agency. But many of those who attend our Sunday Schools wander out and away, unevangelized and unsaved.

Surely there is gross failure somewhere. Why do they not believe the Word of Truth? Is it because they do not hear it? How many teachers and leaders there must be who diligently taught "the Bible," in all orthodoxy perhaps, but who have never presented the personal claims of Christ to their scholars; who have never presented the way of salvation, simply told from a yearning heart to love-hungry boys and girls. How many there must be who, having presented a "plan" of salvation, have never asked those inquiring souls to receive the risen Christ of that plan into their hearts.

It was "Feed my lambs" that the Saviour said to Peter, and through him to the leaders and workers of the church, before His twice-repeated "Feed my sheep" (John 21: 15-17). He is speaking here, not to a father, but to a leader. Boys and girls within the sphere of influence of the church or Sunday School which professes to preach the Word of God surely are the "lambs" for which pastors, Sunday School teachers, and the workers of the church's organized forces must someday give account. What an accounting that will be when Christian leaders and workers stand before their Lord in the day of testing of their service!

It is said that the organized church spends $10,000 to win an adult to Christ. It costs but a few cents, if anything at all, to place the gospel before a child. Giving proper emphasis to the winning of the young, the church could evangelize the world in a generation. There are no better missionaries than the boys and girls. No group of saints as a class is more diligent in soul-winning. None are more faithful and enthusiastic in their confession of Christ than they. Win the boys and girls of America, and this land will be truly Christian in a generation. Win the boys and girls of the world, and the salvation of tomorrow's adults will have been assured.

Let Sunday Schools be evangelistic toward the children! Teaching a Sunday School class is hard work. It is exacting in its demands. It is sometimes laborious. Preparation is often anything but easy. There are days when the teacher becomes so discouraged that the question looms up: "Is it worth the cost?" But it is. There is no work more vital in the organized effort of the church. Its cost is just a faint reflection of its value. To the Sunday School teacher is given a golden opportunity, and with the opportunity goes a grave responsibility.

First Fruits of Today's Reaping

The youngsters won to the Lord in the Sunday School class are themselves a part of the harvest that is already white. Salvation to them is just as real as it is to others much older. But they need not constitute the whole harvest. Win them and they can become the first fruits of a larger ingathering. Win a child and a door is opened that is great and effectual, the door to the home in which his elders live.

How often we have seen the youngster who has come to know the Lord Jesus Christ as his very own personal Saviour influence his family in the direction of the church and Sunday School. Perhaps he doesn't win them to the Lord through his childish testimony, though that happens on occasion; but he opens the door of his household to the tender ministry of the pastor or the callers of the church. Through that open door they may enter in the name of Christ and of His church with the gracious gospel message. There is no surer way into the confidence and affection of the family circle than through the heart of a child. It is so self-evident that we need not pause to prove it, but only call attention to it and challenge you to capitalize upon it.

Your work, then, can be but the beginning of a larger and more far-reaching work continued and brought to completion by the working forces of the church and Sunday School. Your opportunity, you see, is not only to win the child, but to start toward the goal of winning the family of that child.

This great key to Sunday School enlargement—not the only one, it is true, but a great one none the less—is in the hands of the teachers of the Sunday School. One Sunday School of which the writer has personal knowledge took this as a premise and worked accordingly. Teachers of juniors accepted their responsibility to win their charges to the Lord through real heart conversion and regeneration and to do it in their classes. They majored on that one thing. The results were soon evident. Promotion day found a gratifying number of saved boys and girls going into the intermediate department. There was very little numerical loss. Even the places of those who were promoted were filled by incoming juniors, both from the primaries and from the outside.

An unforeseen result was that not only did the next higher department of the Sunday School gain, but also every other department. Most of those juniors had brothers and sisters. They all had older relatives. Many of them had responded to invitations to attend the classes suited to them as junior teachers had called in the homes of their scholars. Many of them, likewise, having heard the gospel, were themselves converted and brought into the fellowship of the church. And it all began when teachers of youngsters bought up their golden opportunity!

The very fact of the Lord's working in the hearts of the children, and the knowledge that souls were being saved served to create a spirit of aggressive evangelism that affected every avenue of the church's ministry. So, you see, your opportunity is not only to win a soul to Christ as you win the child, but to supply the burning coal that can kindle a revival fire.

Laborers for Tomorrow's Harvesting.

But let's go back to the child himself. He has a life before him. It can be a life of Christian service. Whether he spends it in the service of the Lord depends very largely upon whether you win him to the Lord. If you don't do it, there is no assurance that anyone else will. He has a soul to be saved, and as far as you are concerned in the matter there is no one else but you who is in a position to lead him to Calvary.

Build up the child in the faith, once he is saved, and you have a laborer in the Lord's harvest. Call the roll of the greatly-used servants of God. Most of them were won in childhood, and early in life they were brought along the way of growth in grace through the personal ministry of someone else. Take out of the ministry, out of the mission fields, out of the congregations those who were saved and built up in childhood and you would have little left, and that of doubtful immediate usefulness. Let us not limit our view of today's results, but take in to-morrow's as well. When the Lord began a program of calling out a people to His name, He launched a work that was to have results for at least nineteen hundred years!

THE WORLD

We cannot limit the responsibility to parents and Christian leaders. The Lord's people, all of them, are responsible for the winning of the child. In the neighborhood in which Christian homes are established, on the streets where Christians walk, on the vacant lots and playgrounds which Christians pass, thousands of boys and girls are waiting for someone who cares to tell them what God has done for them in Christ and to ask them to receive His salvation.

The lost sheep of Matthew 18:13 is the little one of Matthew 18:14. It is not the Father's will that one of these little, straying, lost sheep should perish. It is for us, His people, to seek them out and bring them to Him and to the company of His people. This we have not done in any great measure. The people of God have failed the world's children.

How shall we gather them in? What agencies shall we use? What forces shall we employ?

No new machinery is needed, but a new determination and a new immediate objective must be supplied. Let parents win their own young. Let the church organize itself for a continuous harvest of souls through the Sunday School and related activities. Let teachers take their duties seriously, placing at the forefront of their ministry the winning of every boy and girl who comes into the Sunday School, even though it be but a casual visit. Let there be unceasing prayer for the "lambs" of the church's field, which is the world.

The Home Bible Club.

One great means the church can employ to reach the unreached, bring them to Christ and develop them in Him and finally to identify them with the church, is through a home Bible club.

Christian homes should be mission points. Into them the unreached boys and girls of surrounding homes should be privileged to come to hear again and again of the love of God and the cleansing power of the blood of Christ. No matter what the prejudice of the homes from which they come, they will come to such a gathering, though they might never set foot inside a church building. There is no greater out-reaching agency which the church may employ than this simple plan of gathering neighborhood boys and girls into a Christian home for an after-school hour of informal Bible study.

The harvest that is being gathered in through home Bible clubs is amazing. Twenty thousand boys and girls in the city of Chicago alone heard the gospel in a single year. Many of these were brought immediately into nearby Sunday Schools. Churches aware of the effectiveness of such a program have added scores of otherwise unreached families to their prospect list. One such reported fifty-two additions to the Sunday School in one season through ten Bible club "outposts." Another found it not unusual to receive twenty new scholars on a single Sunday. One opened one hundred-fifty doors to the calling ministry of the church through eight clubs held for short periods. And many are developing into outpost Sunday

Schools in newly built-up residential sections where churches have yet to be established.

The plan is simple. A day is set. A home opens its doors. A teacher is appointed. The neighborhood is canvassed with the purpose of inviting mothers to permit their children to attend the Bible story hour. Invitations are left for the children themselves. When the day and hour come—the boys and girls are there! It seldom fails!

The hour is spent in singing, learning Scripture passages, praying, and is climaxed by a well-told Bible lesson in story form, usually with the aid of a flannelboard scene to enable the child to visualize the story. From the first session children are evangelized and simple instruction relative to salvation is given them.

Once the denominational barrier is broken down, the way is opened to invite the individual child and his parents and family to visit the Sunday School. Doors fast closed to callers from the church are thus opened, sooner or later.

The Junior Congregation.

More and more the church is realizing that effective work with the children must include, where it is possible, a Sunday morning ministry especially for them. Children get much more than we realize from services and sermons designed for adults, but they will get still more from an hour that is truly theirs, with quarters and furniture suited to their age.

One vacation school specialist insists that the first day be wholly evangelistic in order that the school may have the teaching ministry of the Holy Spirit operative in the scholars so far as possible. His approach is Scripturally sound and his schools are pre-eminently successful.

Special Campaigns.

Every church should conduct special evangelistic campaigns as often as adult campaigns are held. Why not? Specially trained servants of God are available. The children respond astoundingly. The facilities of the church are available. It is a constant source of amazement that such great numbers of boys and girls will attend and answer to the call of the Saviour. Always such special effort results in an immediate upswing in Sunday attendance and interest.

Released Time and Week-day Classes.

The church should neglect no opportunity afforded to gather boys and girls together around the cross and the tomb. A child may enter Sunday School at about the age of four, and drop out at fourteen, thus giving him an average of a ten-year period for religious instruction. Considering that in the average Sunday School he may not receive more than seventeen hours a year of intensive, systematic instruction, the best that we can hope for under those conditions would be one hundred and seventy hours. During the time he is in the Sunday School he would receive twelve thousand hours in the public school under the most favorable conditions for learning.

Twelve thousand hours in the public school! One hundred and seventy hours in the Sunday School! Twelve thousand hours to prepare him for this short, uncertain existence! One hundred and seventy hours to prepare him for eternity!

Open-air Evangelism.

The perennial objection to such work is that little can be done to follow up open-air converts among children. From the human viewpoint that is true. The ever-present problem of how to continue the contact with, and the spiritual development of, the child is never more acute than it is in open-air evangelism. Don't attempt such work if the converts cannot be followed up, say some. Such a conclusion is not sound. That is to say that it is better to permit an unreached child to grow up in an atmosphere of unbelief, with every possibility that he will live and die without Christ, finally to spend eternity in hell, than to bring one to initial faith in Christ and leave him to God without a continuing contact.

Hudson Taylor chose the latter method in his work in China when, despite the arguments of others, he traveled throughout the land giving a simple evangelistic message, winning some and leaving them to God. That God is able to complete that which He has begun in such instances, even though human teachers are not at hand, has been abundantly demonstrated. There was hardly a city in which Hudson Taylor had preached that did not hold converts who had stood true, though spiritually immature and untrained, when his steps were retraced in later years. Heathendom and unreached childhood have much in common in this regard.

No! Let us not evade the issue. Children can be evangelized in the open air. There God can come into their lives. There He can begin a work that will continue until eternity. To the task, then, doing what we can and depending upon God to continue the contact and to provide for the "follow-up."

The greatest mission field in the world touches your doorstep. The most accessible evangelistic harvest to be found anywhere is waiting for you to thrust in the sickle. Childhood is waiting to receive the gospel which you have. That gospel is the power of God, and it is yours to proclaim. Children *will* listen; they *will* believe. God commands and to His command stands ready to add the enablement. Go then, in the strength that God gives and win the children for Christ and bring them up in Him.

"All God's commandments are His enablings," a poet once said. And it is true. The work is His. He stands ready to supply all your needs as you render your obedience to His will. If you are a parent, go now to the child whom God has given you and lead him to your Lord. If you are a leader or worker in the Lord's organized forces, take the yoke in which He now stands waiting and win the young. And whoever you are, if you are a child of God, go to the boys and girls of your neighborhood in whatever way the Lord may indicate for your particular circumstances, and give the gospel to those waiting, trusting souls. "God's commandments are God's enablements."

Notes

Notes

Notes

Notes

Notes

Notes

Notes

Notes

A

Date Due

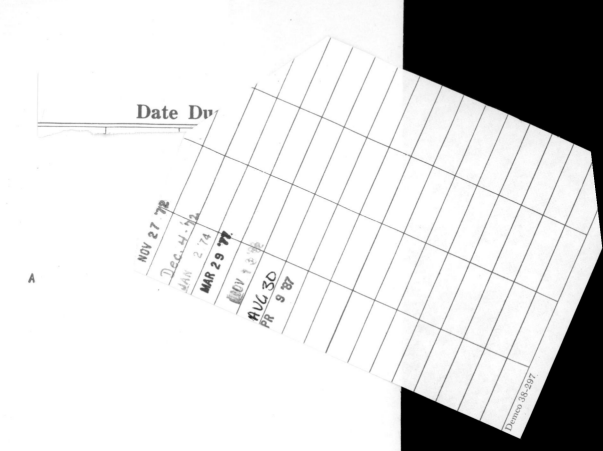